BeYOUtiful

RADIATE CONFIDENCE, CELEBRATE DIFFERENCE & EXPRESS YOURSELF

WRITTEN BY
SHELINA JANMOHAMED

ILLUSTRATED BY
CHANTÉ TIMOTHY

WELBECK

For Hana and Iman, my inspiration and my world. I love you.
And for Maryam, Aamina and Anayis
To all the girls around the world: you are beautiful. Believe it because it really is true.

Acknowledgements: Special thanks to Hajera Memon, Shaheen Bilgrami, Bryony Davies, Chanté Timothy, Hannah Weatherill, Chloe Seager, Alli Brydon, Jo Lal, Welbeck Publishing, Northbank Talent Management, Amatullah, Haleemah, Helen, Sophia. And always to the one and above all the One. SJ

Published in 2022 by Welbeck Children's
An Imprint of Welbeck Children's Limited,
part of Welbeck Publishing Group.
Based in London and Sydney.
www.welbeckpublishing.com

Design and layout © Welbeck Children's Limited 2022
Text © Shelina Janmohamed 2022
Illustrations © Chanté Timothy 2022

A CIP catalogue record for this book is available from the British Library.

ISBN 978-1-78956-295-8

Commissioning Editor: Bryony Davies
Art Editor: Deborah Vickers
Designer: Kathryn Davies
Picture Researcher: Paul Langan
Production: Melanie Robertson

Printed in Heshan, China
10 9 8 7 6 5 4 3 2 1

FSC
www.fsc.org
MIX
Paper from
responsible sources
FSC® C020056

The publishers would like to thank the following sources for their kind permission to reproduce the pictures in this book.
Alamy Stock Image: agefotostock 62; Chronicle 65; colaimages 97; PA Images 70; The Print Collector 37TR; Dom Slike 46
Getty Images: David M Benett 27; Heritage Images 45TR; Anwar Hussein/Wirelmage 69
Natalia Ivanova/The Ethic Origins of Beauty: 78
Shelina Janmohamed: 4, 5
Shutterstock: John Angelillo/UPI 25; ANL 79; Bariskina 80; Matt Baron/BEI 21; Liat Chen/PYMCA 38BR; Neale Cousland 23; Crollalanza 44; Cubankite 40, 57; David Davies/ANL 66; Everett 18BR, 45TL, 67R, 98; FashionStock.com 68; Featureflash Photo Agency 49, 67TL, 74; David Fisher 71; fotokalua 41; Vladimir Gjorgiev 102; Gorodenkoff 101; Granger 17; Zdenko Hirschler 20; Mohamed Hossam/EPA-EFE 73; Kathy Hutchins 12; Nils Jorgensen 13; KELENY 105TR, 105R; Kobal 35; maxfoto.shutter 100; James Mccauley 61; meunierd 42; Moviestore 19BR, 38L; Myskina6 96; panda_o 60; Gaston Piccinetti 34; Eugene Powers 108; ppart 122; Serge Rocco 50; Ryan Rodrick Beiler 39; Lakkana Savaksuriyawong 84; Richard Shotwell/Invision/AP 59; Sipa 33; Snap 19TL; Dietmar Temps 83; Eileen Tweedy 18TL; Universal History Archive/UIG 37BL; Richard Young 47
Every effort has been made to acknowledge correctly and contact the source and/or copyright holder of each picture. Any unintentional errors or omissions will be corrected in future editions of this book.

CONTENTS

HELLO! THIS IS ME...

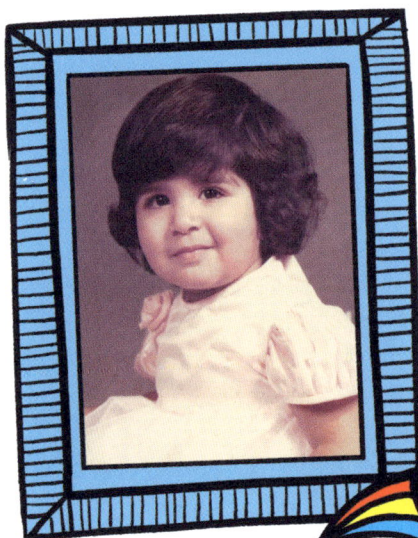

Cute, right? Well, that's what my mum and dad thought. And the picture on the next page is me now. I look quite different, and I suppose that's because I've grown up. I'm still growing in lots of ways, my body is always changing, and my mind is always growing. My mum and dad still think I'm cute, even though I'm much older now. They also still want to squeeze my cheeks, but I don't let them do that anymore. Because it REALLY HURTS.

I'm quite small, brown-skinned and I wear a headscarf, underneath which is long, dark hair. My skin has different shades on different parts of my body. I have skinny legs, knobbly knees and a round, squishy belly. My face has some darker freckles, and there are dark moles and beauty spots scattered across my body. I'm happy with all of that because that's me.

Some days I feel on top of the world about how I look, and some days I want to hide in a cupboard and not let anyone see me. (Top tip: don't hide in a cupboard. But if you do, take snacks, a torch and a good book to read. Like this one.) Sometimes feelings pop into my head by themselves, sometimes they appear because of what other people say, and sometimes I've had those ideas and feelings because of things I've seen or read.

All of this has made me realise one thing: it's normal to think about how we look. It affects how we feel about ourselves and the world around us. If you're reading this book, then I know that you are probably already thinking about what it means to be beautiful, just like I do.

I work in advertising with big companies, including beauty and fashion brands, thinking about the words and pictures used to make adverts. I also write for newspapers and go on TV and radio to discuss ideas about beauty and what makes us who we are. Which means I spend a lot of time thinking about the subject of being beautiful. There are lots of insider secrets that nobody ever tells you. And I think it's about time the truth about being beautiful was shared. Which is why I'm going to sneak you behind the scenes to find out for yourself! I want to share it with you. And hopefully you can share it with others.

So, of all the books you could have picked to talk about what being beautiful means, you chose a good one, because this one will hopefully change your life. At the very least it has some gorgeous pictures, some amazing stories of brilliant women and some very peculiar beauty techniques from history. What could be better?

It took me a long time to work out that there are lots of different ways to be beautiful, and that's what I want to share with you. There isn't a maths or science book that gives you a formula on how to be beautiful. There isn't a recipe book to cook up a perfectly beautiful woman. What it means to be beautiful changes all the time. It's different in different places. Here's the amazing thing that no one ever tells you: there is no single opinion that is right or wrong. There's only one opinion that counts, and that's YOURS!

Lots of love,

Shelina

(Mum of two girls)

5

ABOUT THIS BOOK

First, I'm going to tell you what this book is **not**. It's not about what clothes to wear, or how to put on make-up, or how to strike the perfect pose for a photograph. It's not about how to make yourself what *other* people tell you is "beautiful". It's also not going to tell you that beauty is something we shouldn't think about because it's actually quite normal to think about it. And it's something that **all of us think about**.

This book isn't going to try to pretend that how you feel about the way you look is not important. I know that it's annoying when someone tells you that what's on the outside doesn't matter because **how you feel about yourself is important**, and how you feel about how you look is part of that. People say being beautiful on the inside is what counts. This is definitely true, but it doesn't mean we don't care about what's on the outside.

This book is going to talk about **what it actually means to be beautiful as well as who gets to decide what is beautiful**. You might be surprised to know that there isn't one fixed idea of being beautiful. Since the beginning of human history, people have constantly **changed their minds** about what kinds of looks are beautiful.

Sometimes being beautiful meant being slim – or even stick thin – or it meant the opposite – "voluptuous" (which is a lovely word to describe being round in lots of places). Sometimes people thought high foreheads were attractive and in other times, big eyes were the thing.

People's ideas of what it means to be beautiful **vary by country and culture**, too. So, someone whose picture is on the cover of a beauty magazine in the UK might look totally different from someone on the cover of a beauty magazine in China! In some places, dark skin is considered the most beautiful. In other places, being told you have eyes like a cow used to be considered a compliment! The list could go on...

All of this goes to show that there is **no single description** of what it means to be beautiful. We can't build a robot that everyone, everywhere would agree was beautiful. (A robot wouldn't be beautiful anyway because it doesn't have a real personality.) You're probably going to be able to guess what's coming next. The reason for all this is because...

WE ALL FIND DIFFERENT THINGS BEAUTIFUL!

There isn't one fixed description of being beautiful, and what we think is beautiful can change over time and be different in different places. **So why do some people get called beautiful and not others?**

In this book, we will talk about how much of what we think of as being "beautiful" is **what other people think**. And since other people think different things... is anyone really more beautiful than anyone else at all?

Let's find out...

Get ready!

I can only let you into this book to discover all the secrets I've spent my life investigating if you promise to bring two things with you:

CURIOSITY: Learning about being beautiful actually starts from asking lots of questions. For example: do people have the same ideas everywhere? Who decides about being beautiful? "HOW" and "WHY" are brilliant words: keep them ready.

BELIEF: You have to **believe** you are beautiful. I totally understand that this is a BIG ASK. Don't tell anyone else, but I sometimes struggle with it, too. But trust me on this one. You'll be amazed that as the book carries on, if you start with belief, it will get stronger and stronger.

BELIEVE IN YOUR BODY

Our amazing bodies give us the chance to be part of the world and fulfil our hopes and dreams. On the inside our bodies are all very similar, but on the outside they all look different. From young to old, curvy to skinny to athletic, tall to small, there are so many kinds of bodies with different abilities. And as we grow up, our bodies keep changing, too. One thing is for sure, all of them are beautiful. Let's get exploring and find out what goes on inside our bodies, what ideas people have about them and how to make the most of the incredible bodies that we have.

YOUR BODY AND YOU

Do you have a body? Excellent! Then this book is just for you. Your body can do all sorts of amazing things like breathe, pump blood, digest food, grow hair and smile! It's lucky you have a body, not just because bodies are incredible, but because it means you exist: your own body gives you a place to be you.

You and your body

If you didn't have your body, could you still be you? If you were in a completely different body, would you be a different person? No! **Your body and you are two separate things.**

You are you. Your ideas, dreams, personality and individuality; your imagination, hopes, feelings and so much more... all of these make you the amazing person that you are. Your body is the physical place where all these things happen. It's **where** and **how** you exist in the world. It's how other people see you and interact with you. Most importantly, your body is a place to **express yourself** and **experience life**.

If you didn't have a body, I suppose you'd be a ghost and waft about. You couldn't give hugs, enjoy delicious ice cream, maybe one day go to the moon or achieve any of your dreams. And how boring it would be if your body just walked around with no YOU in it: no personality, no ideas, no thoughts, no imagination? Lucky for you, you have an amazing body, and that, added to your amazing YOU, is **a winning combination**.

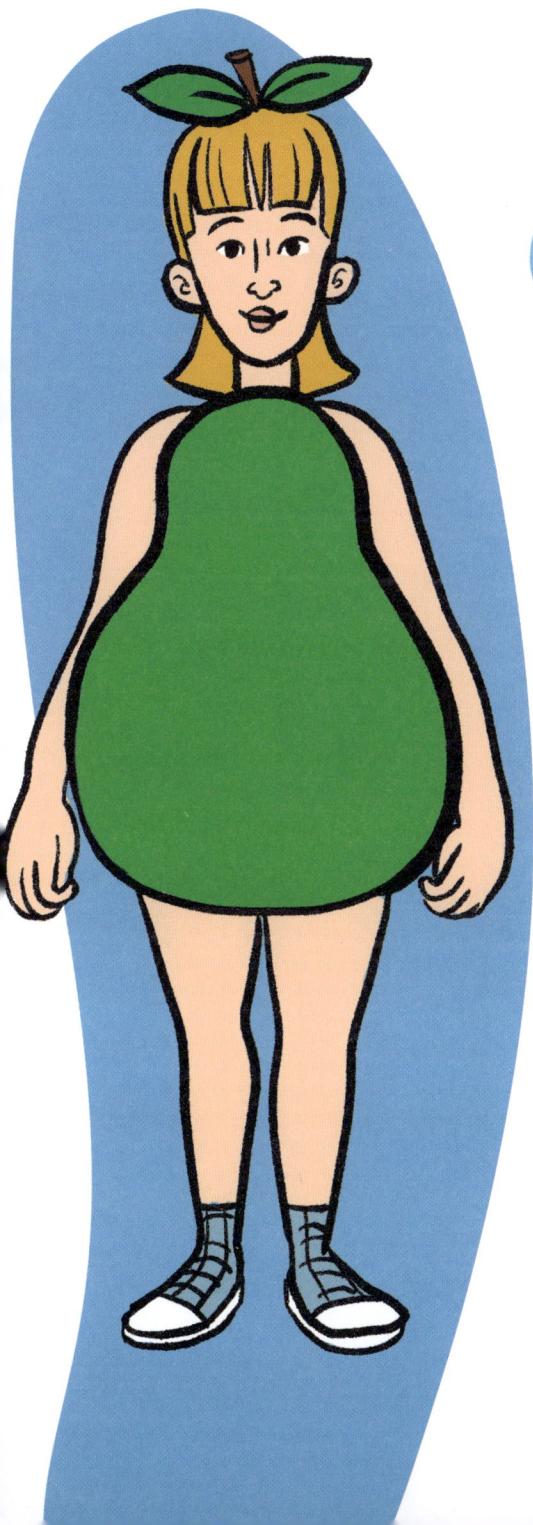

Beautiful, bold, brave and brilliant bodies

There are many amazing things going on inside people's bodies. Blood transports oxygen and nutrients. The brain sends and receives signals for movement and feeling... I could keep going and fill a whole book.

Some bodies are tall, some are small, some round and some skinny. Some are young, some are old, some have bits missing, some have extra bits or bits that don't work quite like anyone else's.

There's no such thing as a "perfect" or "ideal" body. And the opposite is also true – that there is no such thing as a "wrong" or "ugly" body. Bodies are bodies. And in the grand scheme of things, the genetic variation between different bodies is only about 0.1%.

Jyoti Amge

Our bodies vary, and that's normal

Even though bodies are 99.9% all the same, the small things that make them different can sometimes feel big. Take height, for example. There are very tall women and women with dwarfism which makes them smaller than average. Zeng Jinlian was the tallest woman ever recorded at 246.3cm tall, and Jyoti Amge is the smallest at 62.8cm.

Another way people can differ is by being skinny or curvy, or somewhere in between. Bottoms, breasts and tummies can be different shapes and sizes. Facial features vary too, like eyes, noses and face shapes. And bodies change as they age.

Proportions can be different, so some people have longer legs compared to their abdomen, and others have shorter legs (like me!). You might have what you think are small feet or big feet. People from different cultures and heritages might have different body shapes and features.

Someone might have a prosthetic leg, be in a wheelchair or have a cleft lip. You can be flabby or taut, have cellulite or stretch marks, have bits inside you made of metal, or, well, anything! There are so many variations. But they are all bodies!

TILLY LOCKEY

At 15 months old, Tilly Lockey was diagnosed with meningococcal septicaemia (blood poisoning) and had to have both her hands amputated. Now a teenager, she wears bionic hands and campaigns to have the technology available to more children. She's a model, beauty and style influencer and a children's TV presenter.

"I like to think of my hands as a really awesome accessory," Tilly says. "I like to match it with my outfit or how I'm feeling. It's kind of like a handbag that you can just pick up and add to your outfit."

She doesn't think describing someone as disabled is useful. "If you break [the word] apart," she explains, "it's like [saying] you're unable to do things, which I think is completely wrong." "Whether they've got hands or no hands. Or whether they've lost a leg, or whether it's deafness or blindness. At the end of the day, everyone's just the same."

Bodies keep changing

Your body starts by being born, becomes a child, goes through puberty and eventually grows older. Bodies change in many ways. Sometimes bodies get rounder – including growing breasts for girls. Hair grows (sometimes in new and unexpected places!). Female bodies might get pregnant and grow babies. People can even get shorter as they get older!

Body shapes and sizes

Bodies come in different shapes and sizes. FACT. Human beings like to be able to group things together, so some people like to talk about "body shapes". You might see something like the images below in magazines, describing women's bodies as food. I think I'm a cross between a string bean and a peanut.

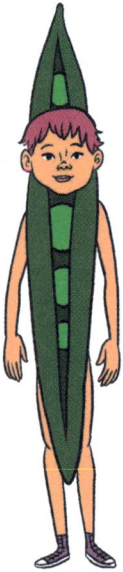 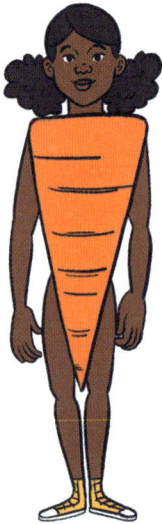   

String bean   Carrot   Peanut   Pear   Apple

How does it make you feel that women's shapes are described with so much detail and are compared to things like fruit? Confused? Enlightened? Hungry? A good reason to identify your body shape is to get to know your own body and be proud of it. What's not a good reason is to feel you have to use clothes to hide your "flaws". There is no such thing as a "perfect" shape, and your shape – whatever it is – isn't flawed. Your body is your body.

Why do body sizes come in numbers?

If women buy clothes today they pick a size, usually a number like 8, 12, 16 or 20. But it wasn't always like this. After the Second World War, the US government conducted a study of 15,000 women. They randomly named sizes in even numbers. Each was based on the measurements of bust, waist, hip and height.

Sizes can be useful, but the measurement and shape of "standard" sizes are just what someone decided. It doesn't mean that the sizes and shapes of clothes are "right" or that your body is "wrong". It's just a way to sell clothes. The first women measured were all white, but women of other heritages have different shapes and sizes. A second group measured later were from the military, so they had a specific kind of body trained for physical combat, which not everyone has. In fact, the "standard sizes" aren't even standard themselves. A size 14 in one shop might be totally different from a size 14 in another. That's confusing!

Some of the size names are peculiar. Size zero is extremely thin. If that's your natural body and you're healthy, that's fine. But many women become ill to achieve a size zero. The opposite is also strange: "plus size". This suggests there's a "right" size and anything more is "plus". Now, you being a clever clogs, you know that there is no "right" size, so it doesn't even make sense to call something "plus"!

The bodies we see around us

Real bodies come in all sorts of shapes and sizes. But for some reason, the bodies usually used to represent all of us are much more limited.

Wouldn't it be wonderful if all the mannequins, pictures, images and models reflected **real women of all races, sizes, ages and abilities**? You can keep going with this list. Because the more kinds of bodies we see around us, the more beauty we can celebrate, and the happier we feel about ourselves. Can you spot how I've tried hard to include all sorts of women in this book?

BODIES THROUGH HISTORY

We're going to jump into a time machine and take a trip back through history. But before we begin, there are a few important questions to consider...

1. How do we know about beauty from the past?
By looking at artwork and very old objects, today's experts have developed theories about what people thought was beautiful in ancient times. From more recent history, clothing, magazines and photos survive. These give us clues about the body shapes, styles and beauty looks women were trying to achieve.

2. Is this what ALL women of that time looked like?
Most of the women in art from the past were wealthy or famous. To commission these paintings, tapestries, sculptures and photographs, a person needed money, so these items don't represent most people. We don't even know if the images show what these people even really looked like, or just how they wanted to be seen! After all, an artist would definitely do their best to make a queen look spectacular in her portrait.

3. Was this the ONLY look considered beautiful?
Ordinary women, who were not wealthy or famous, might have wanted to look like the women they saw in art, but most wouldn't have had the time or money. And the artists of the day probably thought they weren't even worthy of being artistic subjects so all their ways of being beautiful weren't recorded. There were no selfies back then! Like today, chances are there were all sorts of looks, bodies, faces, skin and hair, and all sorts of definitions of being beautiful.

Venus of Willendorf – one of the oldest objects showing a woman

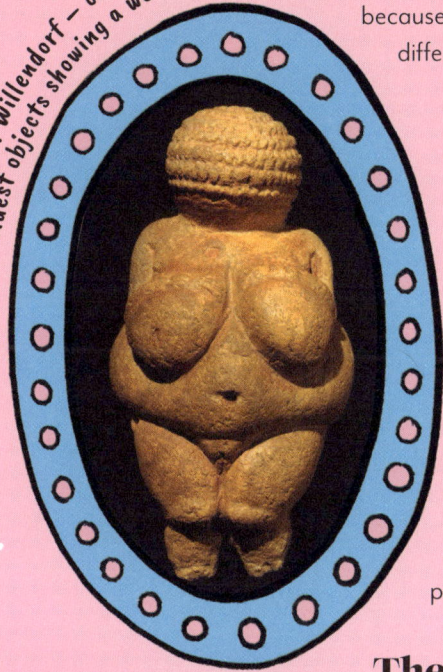

It's time to climb into our time machine. It would be amazing if we could travel through all of time and space, but then this book would be the size of the Universe. So, to get us started, I've created a short journey through Western history. Even then, I haven't been able to include *all* the different cultures within it, but buckle up your seatbelts because there are lots more cultures, heritages and women from different backgrounds later on in the book. Ready?

The Upper Palaeolithic Era

Zooming back 25,000 years, we can examine what might be the first art object featuring the human body. It's round and curvy with no face: the body seems more significant, perhaps because a well-fed body could endure tough conditions. Or maybe she's pregnant because having lots of children to help you was important.

Perhaps the statue is made by a woman herself, celebrating women's beautiful, curved, powerful bodies. A great celebratory tip from our prehistoric sisters!

The Renaissance (15th century)

The artist Raphael paints women as curvy and pale, with flushed cheeks. Raphael himself admits he doesn't paint portraits of real women, he just draws his idea of a beautiful woman! **I wonder, how often do other people decide what a beautiful woman ought to be?**

The Elizabethan era (1558–1603)

The women here appear to have really, REALLY tiny waists. It's all thanks to the invention of corsets. French aristocrat Catherine de Medici had a bizarre idea that "thick waists" should be banned at court. So wealthy women started wearing corsets. They catch on in England, where they are made with iron and called the "Tudor Corset". They are so tight they can even re-shape your spine. OUCH!

The 1600s

The paintings of Flemish artist Peter Paul Rubens feature voluptuous women, with puffy knees and squishy flesh. Everyone LOVES them. A whole artistic style and type of beauty (called "Rubenesque") is named after Rubens and he becomes more important than any of the women he painted!

The Victorian era (1837–1901)

During the reign of Queen Victoria, it's back to corsets and tiny waists, but with fuller figures. The corsets are so restrictive they crush the ribcage and squash your insides.

A Rubens portrait

The 1900s: Gibson girls

Charles Dana Gibson illustrates magazines and creates a new body ideal called the "Gibson girl". Tall, curvy but athletic, with a slim corseted waist, her hair is piled in a soft poufy bun with ringlets escaping. She is fragile yet voluptuous. No wonder she's just a drawing – this feels impossible to achieve in real life! (Like most beauty ideals.)

A Gibson girl

The Roaring Twenties (1920s)

Being thin is IN. Women with curves wear corsets to flatten their bodies. They use another method too, which lasts until today: extreme dieting.

The Second World War (1939–1945)

Money and resources at limited, but women still want to look good. They improvise with what they've got. Curves and waistlines are back. Women repurpose their husbands' suits, so padded shoulders and jackets are in. They also draw lines up the backs of their legs to pretend they're wearing stockings – which are very hard to get hold of!

How brilliant to create a beautiful new look out of what you already have?!

MARLENE DIETRICH

German actor Marlene Dietrich (1901–1992) is one of the highest paid stars of the interwar period. One of her famous looks is a tuxedo – a contrast to the curvy flowing "feminine" look. In 1933, she arrives in Paris wearing trousers, despite a warning that she would be arrested. The police don't actually carry out their threat, but she does cause a stir. She says, "I dress for myself. Not for the image, not for the public, not for fashion, not for men."

The glamour years (1950s)

The war is over, and it's back to full-on glamour. Time and effort are spent on hair, make-up and trying to look like the "perfect" and "womanly" woman. You'll have noticed that this keeps changing its meaning: one minute curves, one minute slim... well, you get it, it keeps changing. Which is why it's good to decide for yourself!

MARILYN MONROE

Actor and model Marilyn Monroe (1926–1962) is thought to be one of the greatest beauties of her time. But she says, "I'm one of the world's most self-conscious people. I really have to struggle." Just like many of us, the way she feels on the inside isn't how others see her.

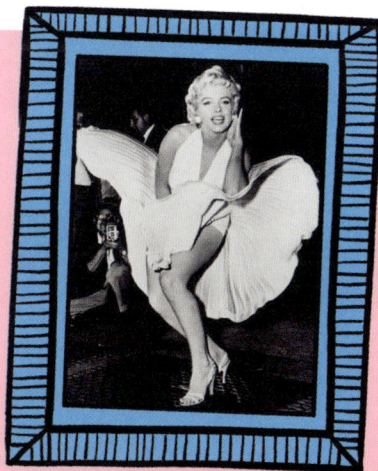

The Swinging Sixties (1960s)

People now say, "the personal is political," meaning that **how your body looks says something about what it means to be a woman or girl**. There's also a growing idea of "Black pride" as a Black cultural movement.

Adverts for dieting are everywhere because women want the skinny look, but this causes illnesses. We flick through magazines featuring the models Twiggy and Jean "the shrimp" Shrimpton – both so called because they are so tiny.

TWIGGY

Twiggy (1949–) is a model, singer and actor. She still models today. When she was young, she thought beauty meant having curves like Marilyn Monroe: "I hated being skinny and funny-looking and desperately wanted a bosom."

People criticised her for being a very skinny model, but that was her natural frame. She made sure to take care of herself. She became an iconic beauty, which goes to show you don't need to look like anyone except yourself, and ideas about beauty can change very quickly!

The 1980s and '90s

In the 1980s, fashion models start to become global celebrities called "supermodels". But looking like tall, skinny supermodels is impossible for the average person. Aerobics classes are all the rage as a way to get that "athletic" look.

But in the 1990s, ideas about beauty start to broaden out, and two main looks are celebrated here as beautiful. There's waif-thin, which we've seen before. And for the first time in the modern era, curvy women.

EMME

Emme (1963–) walked into a modelling agency in 1989 and got signed on the spot, even though her beautiful, curvaceous body was completely different to the models of the time. She went on to be named one of America's 50 most beautiful women by *People* magazine.

When Emme was younger, people criticised her body a lot. But that body was her success. She wrote a letter to her younger self about her body: "It's going to help you build a career. This body is the vehicle that will carry you through the rest of the beautiful, astonishing life ahead of you."

What did we find out on our journey?

1. What was important to people affected what they thought was beautiful.
Philosophers, artists, scientists and all sorts of people shaped ideas. Even now, ideas about beauty are constantly formed by others.

2. Confident and courageous people have introduced new ideas about being beautiful. So when we create our own style, we could actually give other people new ideas!

3. History is hiding incredible stories of amazing women by focusing only on their beauty. To find out their whole stories, we need to go beyond their looks.

OWN YOUR SPACE AND EXPRESS YOURSELF

Your feelings about your body might change all the time. It's perfectly normal to feel positive and excited at times, and worried, unnerved or emotional at others. This is particularly the case as your body grows up and grows older in new and unfamiliar ways. It can be helpful to discuss your feelings with friends or grown-ups.

Body feelings

Adults have feelings about bodies, too, and have good days and bad days, good feelings and bad feelings, confidence and confusion. You can borrow some ideas like these terms to describe how to tackle feelings about your body.

- **Body positivity** is about loving your body and feeling good, whatever your shape, size, height, culture or heritage. (Everyone should feel good!)
- **Body neutrality** is the idea of accepting your body as it is and for what it does because everyone has a body. (Because they do!)

It IS okay to celebrate each other and give positive comments. Use adjectives that feel encouraging. Be kind and reassuring because everyone has worries about how they look.

What is NOT OKAY is "body shaming". That's when you mock or criticise a person's body shape or size and make them feel bad, especially in front of other people. This is a horrible thing to do. As lovely readers of this book, I'm counting on you **never, ever to do this**. If you hear someone else doing it, I'm confident you'll stop them.

There is never any reason to feel ashamed of your body, and anyone who says there is, or makes you feel that way is wrong. Unfortunately, in history and even today, women are often made to think there is something wrong with their bodies just because they are women. We can stop that now. Instead, let's make women and girls proud of our bodies. Let's try saying this: **"Hello Body, I feel good about you, and I'm proud of you. Thanks for all you do."**

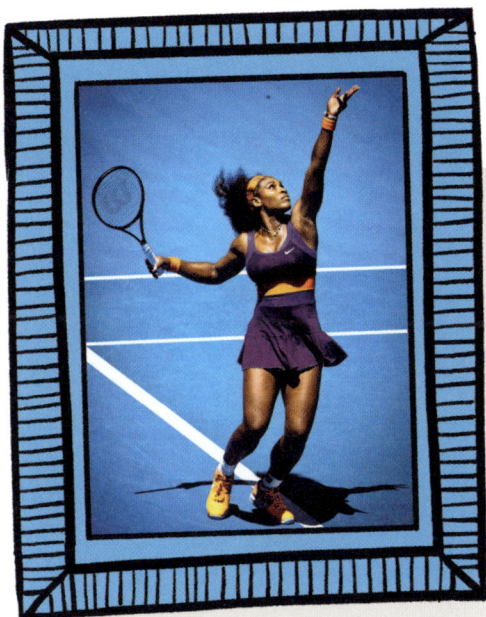

SERENA WILLIAMS

The greatest female tennis player of all time, Serena Williams (1981–) has played professionally for nearly 25 years. She's a businesswoman, actor, charity founder and fashion icon.

She overcame many barriers including all the comments people have made about her body, how she chooses to dress, her hair and even for being Black! She says, "It doesn't matter what your background is or where you come from. If you have dreams and goals that's all that matters."

She uses her body and her style to show who she is. She knows having a strong, powerful, athletic, curvy, sporty body is as beautiful and amazing as any other kind of body. "If we all liked the same thing, it would make the world a really boring place!" she says. "What matters most is that I like myself."

Who is your body for?

YOU! It's a simple answer, but an important one. It's not there for other people to stare at. Or touch. Or stand too close to. Or comment on. It's not there to make other people happy. Or to smile on demand. It's not there to keep other people busy saying mean things. And it's definitely not there to make you feel bad. **Your body is for YOU to enjoy and live your life.**

Who owns your body?

YOU own your body! It sounds simple, doesn't it? And it is. Everything about your body is for you to decide: how you present it, who looks at it, what bits they see, how you feel about it.

Your personal space is an invisible border around you that it is unacceptable to cross. It includes who can stand close to you or touch you. Be careful not to go into someone else's personal space without permission. Your photos are also part of your personal space. So don't show photos if you don't want to, especially if people are trying to force you to share personal pics.

It's NOT OKAY for people to say things that invade your personal space, like mean things but also rude or suggestive comments about your body. It's YOUR BODY. It's your right to have boundaries. Even if it feels difficult to stop someone crossing your boundaries, remember: **Say no to space invaders.**

Body language

How do you present your body in your own space? Try out these two poses. First, hunch over. Now, stand up straight and look ahead.

Did you feel anything different? When you're hunched over, it's like hiding away, but if you stand straight, it communicates confidence. Even if you don't feel it, if you keep practising positive body language, you will feel **more and more confident**.

Fabulous fashion

You can use fashion to make a statement about a political idea, to connect with your culture or religion or just to show that you love wearing different looks. Designing and producing clothes is a form of creativity, and how you put an outfit together is, too.

Some people find great joy in wearing the latest fashions, and others see clothes as just something that needs to be done. Ask a grown-up to show you their photos and talk about how their fashion choices changed over time and why.

MADELINE STUART

"When I was 17," said Madeline Stuart (1996–), "I went to my first fashion show. I fell completely in love with beauty and fashion and it was all I have ever wanted to do since." Sometimes called the world's first famous model with Down's Syndrome, Madeline says people treat her differently: "I want to change the way society views people with Down's Syndrome or any disability."

Madeline has successfully walked on catwalks around the world and appeared in magazines. She advises: "If you have your mindset on something, you can achieve it. There is always a way. You need to work hard and be determined. Everyone faces challenges, but overcoming those is what makes us stronger. Believing in yourself is so important!"

Look after your body

Healthy, loved and well-taken care of bodies positively affect our mental health. They make us happier. This makes our bodies happier, which gives us energy to do the things we want to do. An unhealthy body is a sad body. Unhealthy means any kind of extreme. Too much food or too little food, for example, are both unhealthy. If your body is sad, you feel sad.

When somebody says something negative, it can damage this positive cycle. **Don't let negative people or your own negative thoughts stop you from being YOU and from living your life!**

Healthy body   +   Healthy mind   =   Happy life

Focus on face

When it comes to beauty, our face is one of the biggest things we think about. But does the "perfect" or the "most beautiful" face exist? You can probably guess the answer: NO! That's because what counts as a beautiful face changes ALL. THE. TIME. And it's different in EVERY. PLACE. AND. CULTURE. It also depends on the person looking.

"Beauty lies in the eye of the beholder."

ENGLISH PROVERB

In Arabic poetry from around the 5th century CE, a beautiful woman was often compared to a wild cow! The poetry reflected the experiences of the Bedouin Arabs who lived in the desert. Cows were important so they were considered beautiful. In fact saying, "You're such a cow!" would be a compliment. (I don't recommend it now.)

Eyes, their colour and shape all vary, as do our noses, and we use funny descriptions for them like "button" or "aquiline". My mum says mine has a marble in it, just like hers. Ears, mouths, lips, teeth also – guess what! – come in all shapes and sizes, as do jawlines and cheekbones.

Your facial expressions are one of the most amazing things about your face. Raise an eyebrow, do a cheeky wink, try a thinking face... Can you do a crying laughing emoji face? We can be particularly sensitive about our smile. But the important thing is TO SMILE. Studies show that if YOU smile, not only does the person seeing you feel better, **you feel better, too**.

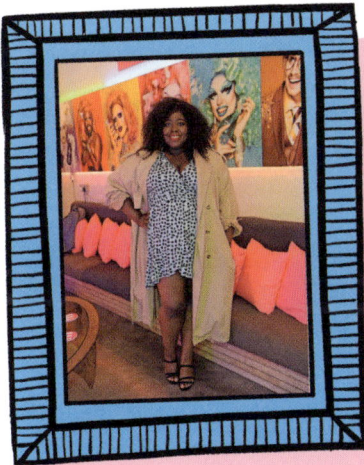

STEPHANIE YEBOAH

As a teenager, Stephanie (1989–) tried to change her body because she faced bullying for it. By doing that she made herself ill. Today she is an author, brand ambassador and public speaker.

"I wasn't doing any of it for myself... I was doing it because I just wanted the policing to stop," she says. She realised that her body was actually looking after *her*, so she set about "apologising TO my body, instead of apologising FOR my body."

She says "fat" shouldn't be used as an insult: it's just a "descriptive word for a body shape... It is society that needs to change its narrow-minded idea of what beauty is."

Changing your body for yourself and for others

Throughout history women have spent time and money, and even risked injury and death, in pursuit of the "perfect" body. As you know by now, there is no such thing. But there are changes you can make – some healthy (yay!) and some dangerous (boo):

Clothes are a way to change how you present yourself and how you appear to others.

Exercise gets your body into good shape and creates positive energy, but as with all things, it should be done in a moderate and healthy way.

Eating healthy, balanced and well-sized meals is important. Extreme dieting or weight-loss products can be very dangerous. Be careful, dieting can start slowly and, without you realising, can become dangerous for your physical and mental health.

Plastic surgery was originally invented to solve medical issues, and is still important for those reasons. But plastic surgery for cosmetic reasons permanently changes your body and carries a risk of medical complications. It may not even get you the result you want. Sometimes it doesn't fix the sadness inside because something else is causing that. So before you make any permanent change, explore the root of your feelings.

Before doing anything about your body shape, whether temporary or permanent, ask yourself:

- **Is it safe and healthy?**
- **Is it right for me?**
- **Is it because I really want to do it, or am I doing it because of what someone else says?**

Because your eyes see beautifully

In the Persian language, if someone gives you a compliment, you can answer, "It's because your eyes see beautifully." It's YOU that decides what is beautiful and makes it so. And that's the whole point of this book – to recalibrate our eyes to see the beauty in ourselves and all around us. **We can choose to see beautifully.**

Your body is phenomenal

Your body is unbelievably, incomparably, outrageously, fantastically amazing. And beautiful. Yes, YOUR body. So, trying hard not to roll your eyes, but genuinely believing it because it's completely and totally true, let's say the most important thing together: **"I love my body."**

Did you say it? Did you mean it? Let's try again, and this time you can shout it out:

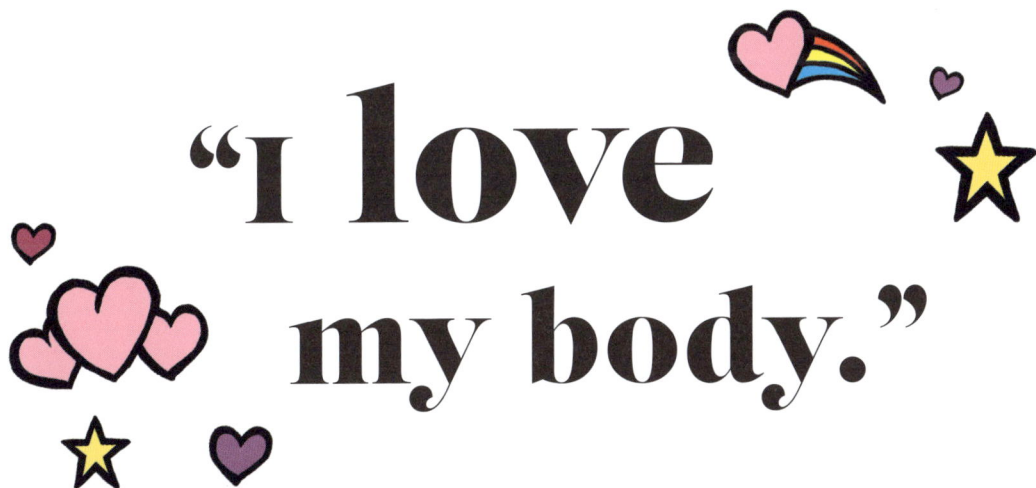

"I love my body."

CELEBRATE YOUR HAIR

People have different ideas about what kind of hair is beautiful, and women use their hair to express themselves in lots of different ways. Rapunzel had long blonde hair. Beyoncé has thick dark hair, sometimes in an afro. My favourite fictional hero is Anne of Green Gables, famous for her red hair! I cover my hair when I'm outside the house, but when I'm in private it's long, thick and dark, and I love styling it. Your hair tells your own personal story.

ALL ABOUT HAIR

In 2004, the longest hair ever documented was measured. It belonged to Xie Qiuping from China and was 5.60 metres long, which is nearly as tall as a bus. That's a lot of hair! Your head probably has around 90,000 to 150,000 hairs growing on it. Fancy counting them? The hairs will stay on your head for between two and seven years before they fall out and new ones grow in their place. You lose about 50 to 100 strands per day.

What is hair and how does it grow?

Hair is made of a protein called keratin. It grows from the root below the skin and up through a **follicle** (a little tube the hair comes through). When hair passes through the skin's surface, the cells that make up the hair die. That's why it hurts to pull out your hair from the root, but it doesn't hurt to get a haircut.

Hair can be thick, fine, curly, straight, wavy, frizzy... it's all down to the shape of your follicles. These different thicknesses and textures can completely change the way hair looks, how it grows and how you style it. You can't force one type of hair to go into a style that only suits a totally different type of hair.

Hair colour

The melanin in hair is what gives it its colour, and your genes decide the amount of melanin you have. Black hair contains the most melanin and white hair contains the least. Globally, black is the most common hair colour and red is the rarest.

People often try to give different meanings to different hair colours, as if your hair affects your personality. (It doesn't.) Words are used to try and create emotions about different colours, like platinum blonde, mousey brown or fiery red.

LILY COLE

The supermodel and actor Lily Cole (1987–) had self-doubt as a child. "I hadn't considered myself attractive." She says about her red hair, "When I'd meet people, I would think they wouldn't like me – because I'm a redhead. It's absolutely absurd! The irony is that now I love my hair." Lily got straight As in her A levels and graduated in History of Art from Cambridge University. She founded a technology start up called Impossible to bring more kindness to the world.

White and grey hair are the subject of much discussion. In some cultures they can be considered a sign of wisdom. In others they are seen as a sign of age and something to be hidden. Sometimes it can be fashionable to deliberately dye hair grey. The truth is, no colour is better or worse. Anyone who says mean things about someone's hair colour doesn't know that it's all just melanin, and that all hair colours are equally gorgeous.

Hair dye

Dying your hair is nothing new. Natural hair colourings like henna and turmeric have been used for a long time, along with crushed insects like cochineal. In Europe during the 1600s, toxic lead, sulphur and quicklime were used – but you could die of poisoning as a result. The Himba tribe of Namibia use a paste made of ochre minerals and fat called *otjize* to tint their hair and skin red.

A person from the Himba tribe

Hair is personal

Hair gives us each our own individual look. It holds exciting information about what we have eaten and drunk, the specific environment we live in as well as our genetic heritage. Which means our hair tells our unique individual story about the cultures we are part of and our history. Add to that the way we style our hair, and we can say our hair expresses who we are and what we think about the world.

Hair is very personal and is part of our personal space. It is very closely tied to our identity, and can be a sensitive subject. So it's important we respect our own hair and that of others, that we talk about it positively and respectfully and that we don't touch anyone's hair or pry about covered hair, even if it looks different to our own.

FARRAH FAWCETT

The star of an iconic 1970s TV series called "Charlie's Angels" about three crime-fighting women, Farrah (1947–2009) was famous for her signature hairstyle which became known as the "Farrah Flick". When she was diagnosed with cancer, she filmed herself shaving off her famous hair, which was falling out due to chemotherapy. Her bravery was her beauty, and an inspiration.

Bad hair day

People often want to have the hair that they don't have. And it's perfectly normal to have mixed feelings about your hair. Some days you love it, some days you might hate it, some days you have no feelings about it and just get on with your life. When we're having a Good Hair Day, we feel great about ourselves. And when it's a Bad Hair Day, we can feel frustrated or sorry for ourselves. Both of these kinds of days are completely normal.

The problem is we can feel that a Bad Hair Day equals a bad day, as though our body is not on our side. This is made worse if we think our hair doesn't meet the beauty ideals of what hair is "supposed" to look like. But if your hair is misbehaving, that's just naughty hair. It doesn't reflect on you as a person. The thing is, the hair we have is the hair we have. **Love your hair – it's beautiful, it's you, it's your expression.**

If someone judges who you are as a person based on the kind of hair that you have, ignore them. Having the confidence to express your personal, family, cultural, religious or group identity through your hair is something to be proud of.

HAIR THROUGH HISTORY

Let's get back into our time machine and look at hair fashions through history. They change all the time, including in our own lifetimes. Ask an adult about the history of their own hairstyles. They've probably got some funny stories about styles that they thought were fashionable then, but think are terrible now!

Ancient Greece (c1200BCE–323BCE)

Golden or red hair is seen as beautiful. Women pour vinegar on their hair and spend hours sitting in the sun to lighten it. Long hair is a symbol of femininity, health, social status and wealth. It shows you're eating well and have lots of time to style your hair. In contrast, enslaved women who look after these wealthy women often have short, dark hair.

Across the women's faces is a unibrow, seen as a sign of intelligence. Women dab black powder on their eyebrows to make them stand out as much as possible. Or they might collect goat hair, dye it black and then attach it to their faces using tree resin.

Ancient China (c1600BCE–221BCE)

Hairstyles are so elaborate in ancient China that women sleep on a *takamakura*, which is a wooden prop to support the neck and ensure the hairstyle stays intact, even while they sleep. Sounds uncomfortable!

Europe in the Middle Ages (5th–late 15th centuries)

What's that whiff in the air? Nope, it isn't a new-fangled perfume... it's sheep urine women pour on their hair to turn it blonde and achieve a fashionable "flaxen" colour.

High foreheads are THE THING. Eyebrows are almost non-existent so foreheads appear bigger. And hair is plucked from the hairline to make foreheads bigger still. Ouch. The Church doesn't like this, but says that if husbands like their wives to pluck the hair and have big foreheads, then they'll allow it. **Maybe all of them ought to just let the women decide for themselves, eh?** Now there's an idea!

Lady in Red portrait

QUEEN ELIZABETH I

Before Queen Elizabeth I (1558–1603), red hair was extremely undesirable, thought of as villainous or somehow bad. In paintings it was the hair colour given to traitors or barbarians. But Elizabeth made it into the most desirable look of the day, considered beautiful and powerful. Everybody copied her! Even men dyed their beards red. Which just shows that if you're confident in your look, other people will change their ideas of beauty.

Georgian hair (1714–1837)

Towering hair-dos are all the rage for wealthy women. They have the money to pay hairdressers and buy expensive hair products. Often they invite people to watch them having their hair done, and even better – have an artist paint them mid hair-do!

Bring on the bob (1920s)

As ideas change about the role of women, so do ideas about hair length. In the late 1800s and early 1900s, it was fashionable to have long hair, artfully pinned up, taking time, effort and money to look after. But in the 1920s, it's all about the bob, which later inspires the pixie cut of the 1950s and 1960s. All these periods are times of great social change, and **hairstyles that break convention in a radical way are a reflection of that**.

COLLEEN MOORE

The American silent film actor (1899–1988) invented the bob. Her bold hair influence has lasted till today. She loved her bob so much she kept it till she died in 1988. Which just goes to show that if you love a look, and it loves you, why change it?

Punk! (1970s and '80s)

It's time to rebel against the establishment. Bright, colourful, strong haircuts break hair rules. Whether short, spiked or shaved, bright neon or jet black, punk music and fashion is in your face with styles like mohicans. **Hair is there to show you don't care!**

A bold mohican

DIFFERENT APPROACHES

Hair reflects our different cultures and religions and is built on rituals handed down the generations. Whether it's no hair, wrapped hair, covered hair, braided hair or natural hair... the list is endless.

Nuns usually cover their hair

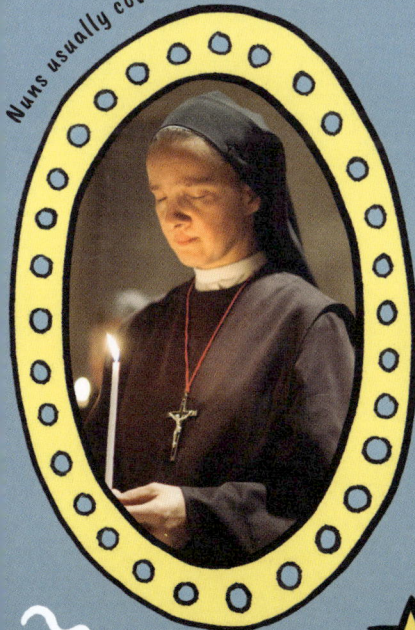

Religion, culture and beliefs

Often, people's religion is the foundation for their ideas about hair. Some devout Sikhs believe neither men nor women should cut their hair, and women aren't to shave, pluck or even trim their brows. Cutting hair is believed to inhibit spiritual development and lead to poor health. For some Hindus, hair – especially women's hair – is a source of spiritual power, and having long hair is a special status for married women.

Some orthodox Jewish women believe their hair should be covered after they get married. A head covering called a tichel or a wig called a sheitel can be used. Christian nuns, who are seen as married to God, may wear a habit to cover their hair.

39

Hijab chic

When in public, some Muslim women cover their hair with a headscarf, sometimes called a hijab. Their hair is considered private, part of their personal space. They believe covering hair is part of dressing modestly, their way of being beautiful. Not all Muslim women cover their hair, but when they do, you'll see all sorts of styles and colours depending on their personal look, as well as local fashion and culture. These include turbans, wraps, burkas, dupattas, tudungs and other variations. At home or with other women, they don't cover their hair, and they try out different styles and fashions just like everyone else!

During the 20th and 21st centuries, Muslim women started reclaiming their headscarves and hair covering as part of their identity, although hair covering goes back thousands of years. In the 2020s, France passed a law banning the hijab in public for under 18s. Many protested by wearing their hijabs, using the hashtag #HandsOffMyHijab.

HALIMA ADEN

Halima (1997–) was the first hijabi Muslim woman on the front of *Vogue* magazine. She has tried out many different looks with her headscarf, but she says she was truest to herself when she wore the black headscarf that she chose for herself, rather than conforming to other people's ideas of what a Muslim woman should look like. "I couldn't wait to start wearing the hijab. Now it's become part of me. It symbolises my faith... It's also a fashion accessory and typically what I plan my entire look around."

Covering your hair

Covering hair can also be part of culture, tradition or simply a way of styling or protecting hair. Places like Japan, Turkey, Eastern Europe, the Philippines and many more have traditions of covering. In many African traditions, headwraps are used in a variety of styles, colours and prints. Even the British Queen sometimes sports a headscarf!

Hair wraps can look after and celebrate hair

Wigs

Wigs can be a way to cover natural hair as well as a lack of hair. Wigs were often worn in history as a status symbol. They are an easy way to change your look temporarily. In France during the era of King Louis XIII, they were made of animal hair and then powdered to make them smell better and keep parasites away.

Hair intuition

Some people believe hair gives us a sixth sense and is another part of our nervous system. Some groups of Native Americans feel that long hair acts as a sort of antenna, like whiskers on a cat. Think about the sensation you get when your hairs stand on end... This usually happens when you instinctively know that something is not right. What are your hairs trying to tell you?

No hair

Sometimes women and girls have no hair. It can be for genetic, age, medical, cultural or religious reasons or simply be an expression of personal style. In fact, having no hair can be as much of a statement as a radical hairstyle. The Maasai women of Tanzania and Kenya shave their head hair and adorn themselves with jewellery to show their cultural identity. Their female beauty standards involve the sleekness of the head.

Maasai tribe

Hindu male and female children go through a head-shaving ritual called Chudakarana for purification, and adults sacrifice hair at temples in exchange for blessings.

Losing hair can be a part of aging. Some people lose their hair as a side effect of medical treatment like chemotherapy or an illness such as alopecia. They can find this very difficult, so it's important to show support.

BLACK HAIR

Black hair can be styled in lots of different ways. These include weaves, coils, braids, dreadlocks, lochs, afros, cornrows, bantu knots, Jheri curls and twists. It's important to recognise that Black hair should be celebrated and can be styled to look however Black women want it to look.

The Natural Hair Movement

The Natural Hair Movement started in the 1960s. It said that wearing Black hair just as it is was beautiful. The hairstyles it supported were a symbol of a bigger protest against racism, saying that "Black is Beautiful" because all colours and types of hair are equal.

The afro of civil rights activist Angela Davis came to symbolise the movement. She says that the style wasn't about fashion, but about "liberation". It is good that ideas are changing to accept all kinds of hair. Wouldn't it be lovely to see more of these styles in the images that are all around us?

43

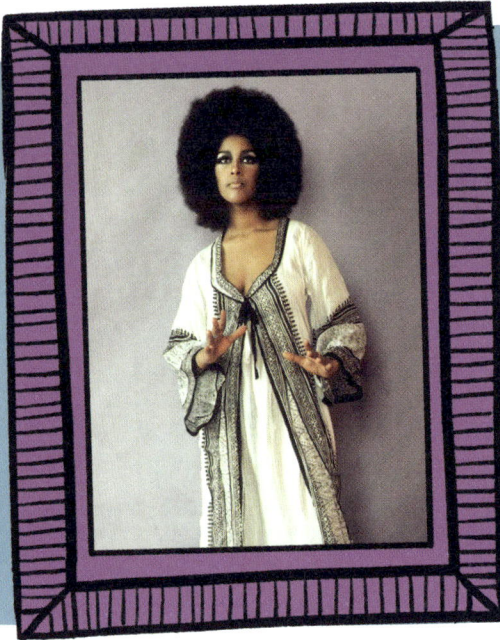

MARSHA HUNT

Marsha (1946–) was the first Black woman to be on the cover of England's high fashion magazine, *Queen*. She was famous for her afro, which was called "The Natural". Marsha is also a novelist, singer and model, and she set up a literary prize to recognise the talents of Black Britons.

Racism and texturism

In the skin chapter you will learn about how racism often suggests that whiter or paler skin is more beautiful. (WRONG!) The same wrong-headed ideas are sadly applied to hair, to say that Black hair is "wrong". Because of such ideas, as well as strict laws and even punishments for having natural Black hair, some Black women might feel compelled to smooth or relax their hair and texture to fit in (and be bullied if they don't). If that's the style they want, that's great, but **no one should feel forced to style their hair in a particular way**.

Unfortunately, along with racism, texturism exists in Black hair. This is when "looser" curls are considered to be more beautiful than tighter ones. **The simple truth is that all of them are as beautiful as each other.**

Black women's hairstyles are integral to culture and history. Some Black women want to reclaim their heritage to show how they are part of it. For example, during the slave trade, traffickers would shave enslaved women's heads to strip them of their identity and humanity, so braids were a protest and a form of beauty. The braids could even map routes to freedom.

CJ Walker

Poro College – a beauty school set up by Annie Malone in Chicago, USA

CJ WALKER AND ANNIE MALONE

Growing up in the United States at the end of the 19th century, CJ Walker (1867–1919) and Annie Malone (1869–1967) suffered many hair and scalp ailments common to Black women at the time, such as baldness, dandruff and burnt and damaged skin. Some of this was due to harsh products not suited to Black hair. So they each started their own lines of haircare products for Black hair – something no one had thought of before – making them among the first self-made millionaires in the USA.

FACIAL AND BODY HAIR

I'm going to tell you a HUGE secret. I mean HUUUUUGE. Everybody, EVERYBODY, I mean EVERY. BODY. has facial and body hair. It's true. Actually, it's not a secret. Everyone knows it. But for some reason we don't talk about it. Weird, huh? If something is part of our bodies, it's natural. And so it's normal to discuss it.

It's everywhere

Some of it might be very fine or it might be thicker. It could be lighter or darker and so more visible or less visible depending on your skin colour. But it's definitely there! On your arms, legs, tummy, your back, upper lip, chin, even on your bottom! As you grow up it appears in new places, including your armpits.

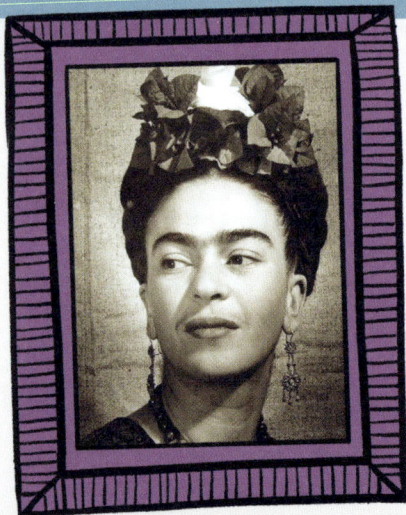

FRIDA KAHLO

The Mexican artist Frida Kahlo (1907–1954) is famous for her self-portraits. She had a thick unibrow, and made it even thicker using an eyebrow pencil. She also had a moustache and armpit and leg hair. She is considered one of the greatest artists of the 20th century and a great beauty. She said: "The most important part of the body is the brain. Of my face, I like the eyebrows and eyes."

How many eyebrows?

You might have two defined eyebrows or one long, connected eyebrow, sometimes called a monobrow or unibrow. It's nothing to do with being more or less beautiful, nothing to do with how nice you are as a person. It's just simple genetics.

What to do with it?

Having facial and body hair or not having it doesn't have anything to do with being womanly or beautiful. (Who decided it was?) Some women love to leave body and facial hair as it is. Others prefer to remove it. Some people's body hair is more visible than others, but if only everyone realised this then we wouldn't all have to pretend that it's anything except completely normal. There is absolutely nothing wrong with body or facial hair. You might like to trim or remove hair in those places where it can get sweaty, but really, apart from that, it's up to you!

HARNAAM KAUR

Harnaam (1990–) is a model, motivational speaker and anti-bullying advocate. She works on spreading self-esteem and acceptance. Her facial hair is caused by the medical condition Polycystic Ovary Syndrome which causes hormonal imbalances. She says: "My body, my rules. If keeping your hair makes you uncomfortable or depressed, then get rid of it; otherwise, if you've got it, rock it," adding, "you can be different and beautiful at the same time."

EXPRESS YOURSELF

One of the brilliant things about hair and head coverings is that, if you want to, you can reinvent your look all the time. You might want to try out a new look in a quick, easy and reversible way. You might want to use them to make a statement to the world about something you believe in.

Be you

We all start out with different kinds of hair, which is why we have different kinds of styles and looks, all of which are beautiful in their own way. The best hair is hair that is well cared for and which is used to express who you are, not hair that tries to copy someone else. You can explore different styles, cuts, colours and accessories to create the look for you: you can cut it, shape it, curl it, straighten it, colour it, bleach it, make it stick up, flatten it, cover it... (although be careful of damaging your hair!).

Hair gives us a sense of our identity and can even be the way people recognise us. Which is why wigs make such good disguises! Hair is about having fun. Hair is a place you can explore your personality and express yourself. You might even create your own signature style – people see you and recognise your haircut! YOU decide what you want to do.

BEYONCÉ

The award-winning American singer and businesswoman (1981–) is constantly reinventing her look. She created a video called "Pretty Hurts", talking about the pressure on women to be beautiful according to someone else's idea of beauty. But she says, "It's really finding yourself that brings you happiness."

Look after your hair

Your hair protects you, loves you, carries your story with you and can express how you feel about the world and yourself, so look after it. Whatever you want to do with your hair, or whatever look you aspire to, the important thing is to know what type of hair you have and therefore **exactly the right way to care for it.** Choose a style that works for your hair. That could be putting it into braids or lochs, or keeping your curls well-moisturised and tangle-free. Or you may prefer to have it short or have no hair at all. It's entirely up to you. All of this applies to women who cover their hair too, like me!

Look after your scalp, and if you try out different colours, ensure your hair is healthy so that it can be resilient. Constant hair colouring can cause damage. What you eat and drink also affects your hair, and a healthy, balanced diet will help. Crash dieting can even cause temporary hair loss!

Keep it clean

Most importantly, keep your hair clean and hygienic. How you do this differs according to your hair type, so it is worth getting advice from someone with similar hair to yours. What I would definitely avoid doing is what a 16th-century doctor recommended would restore your hair: applying boiled slugs, olive oil, honey, saffron, soap and cumin to the scalp. Yuck!

JANE FONDA

The award-winning actor, political activist and beauty icon (1937–) has had some of the world's best-known hairstyles. Her haircut from the film *Barbarella* sparked a new look. Then, as an anti-war campaigner in the 1970s, her "mug shot" when arrested by the police became famous. She says: "I didn't realise this haircut was going to be so iconic – I just thought, 'I can handle this on the front lines.'"

In 1982 she created the first ever celebrity fitness video with a new hairstyle. She gave all the money from the video to supporting the environment. In her 80s – with her stylish grey hair – she is protesting to save the environment! "I tell you, I'm so happy I let it go grey!"

A hair revolution

Hair expresses who we are and our beliefs about the world. It's a place where revolutions can happen because instead of conforming to the rules, hair can be used to break them.

Think of your eyebrows and how they help you give non-verbal clues, moving around to show different expressions, like a (not so) secret language! It's great fun to use them to say things without words! My favourite eyebrow expression is raising one eyebrow to give a clue I'm about to say something really important. Which is happening exactly now...

My raised eyebrow says: my hair is beautiful. It carries in it my past and my heritage. I'm proud of that story of me. And now, it is my way of expressing who I am today. **Why not stand in front of a mirror, raise your own eyebrow and try saying this: "I love my amazing, unique, individual hair!"**

LOVE THE SKIN YOU'RE IN

People have all different kinds of skin, and we have a lot of it, so no wonder we think about it a lot! It's a big part of how the world sees us, and how we see ourselves. Skin is extremely personal. That's why we can be very sensitive about it. But we should be proud of our skin and stand up for it – after all, it's standing up for us and keeping us safe and healthy. That's why people say, "Don't let them get under your skin!" We'll look at the different ways skin looks, feels and changes over time for different people. We will also explore how we feel about our skin and how we can express ourselves through our skin in the most beautiful ways. After all, we want to love the skin we're in!

YOU AND YOUR SKIN

Skin is the biggest organ of your body. It stops everything on the inside falling out, and bad things on the outside getting in. When you're hot, it cools you down by sweating, and when you're cold it helps you stay warm with goosebumps. It helps you avoid danger by sensing heat or something sharp. It has feelings like ticklish, smooth, rough, elastic and, of course, happiness when you're hugged or kissed by someone you love. Amazingly, it can even fix itself if it's damaged.

Superhero skin

Your skin is constantly changing. New cells are born, and dead cells fall off. (Disgusting fact alert: you shed 30,000 to 40,000 dead skin cells every minute. Some of it even collects in your mattress.)

What can it do?

Just a few millimetres thick, skin does a lot of amazing things.

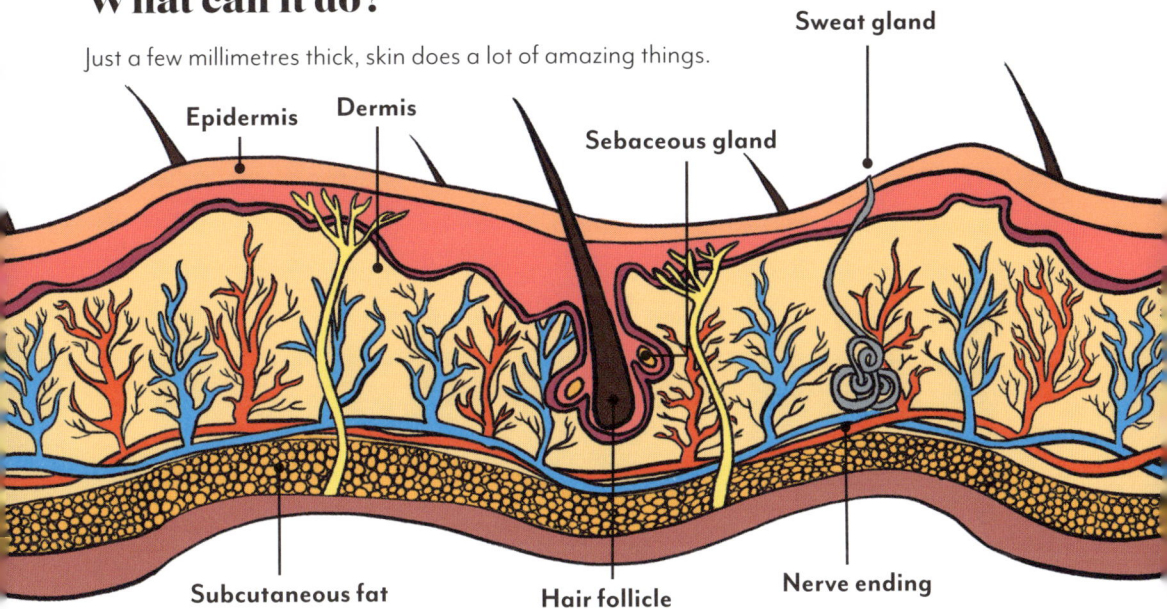

The **epidermis** is the outer layer of skin. It makes new skin cells and contains melanin, which protects skin from ultraviolet light and gives it its colour. Special cells here also help your immune system by fighting infections trying to get into your body.

The **dermis** is the next layer down and contains **nerve endings**, blood vessels, oil glands and sweat glands. Nerve endings help you feel things like heat, cold and pressure.

Sweat glands in the dermis layer pass cooling sweat through little tubes and out of holes called pores which change in size due to heat.

Sebaceous glands produce oil called sebum, which makes skin waterproof and keeps it soft so it doesn't crack, bleed or allow infection in.

Hair follicles grow in the dermis, all over your skin. When you're cold or scared, the muscle around the hair root tightens and you get goosebumps.

Subcutaneous fat attaches your dermis to your muscles and bones. This "under the skin fat" makes sure your skeleton and muscles don't float about and gives important padding to protect them from bumps and falls.

The meaning of the skin you're in

You've probably heard the saying "Be comfortable in your own skin". Being in your own skin is literally the best and most beautiful place to be. Because, apart from anything else, if you were outside your skin, you would be a pile of jelly and bones and it would be very hard to walk anywhere. Or put on any clothes. Or eat ice cream. (I like ice cream.)

Sometimes people say your skin is too light, too dark, too freckly, too plain, too wrinkly or too smooth, that you're wearing too much make-up or not enough make-up... YAWN! It's tiring isn't it, when people have opinions that you never asked for?

The trouble is sometimes people want to change their skin because other people say things that make them feel worried or ashamed of how they look. Someone might claim (completely wrongly!) that because their skin is different to yours they are better than you or you are a bad person. NOT NICE. And NOT TRUE. This is all the proof you need that the kind of skin someone has on the outside doesn't tell us about what someone is like on the inside.

Your skin, nobody else's

Nobody has a right to your skin. Whether that's seeing it (some people prefer to cover their skin), touching it or making comments about it. It's your skin, nobody else's. Nobody has a right to tell you that their skin is better than yours. It isn't. Young, old, dark, light, in-between, freckled, scarred, wrinkled, stretched or pimpled, bumpy with cellulite or smooth, your skin is as important, as human and as equal as anyone else's.

You must be kind and respectful of all kinds of people because they all have feelings about their skin. You should help everyone feel good in their skin and that includes ensuring you feel good about yourself.

AMANDA SEYFRIED

The actor, model and singer Amanda Seyfried (1985–) knows she is more than her looks, but she says, "I was made fun of at school for being pale and ugly." Her advice includes not letting people control your image and your own self-esteem. "Don't let anybody put you in a box. You don't have to listen to those mean girls. They're just there to make you upset and feel bad about yourself and you know, inside, they feel bad about themselves, too. But they don't wanna admit it to anybody."

In her spare time, Amanda works for a charity that helps refugee children injured as a result of conflict.

Marvellous melanin

Your skin absorbs ultraviolet (UV) light which is crucial to your health. It produces Vitamin D which absorbs calcium into our blood. Calcium strengthens bones, teeth and nails, and ensures the health of our muscles and immune system. But too much UV light is damaging, which is where melanin comes in.

Melanin is a pigment produced by melanocyte skin cells. It prevents skin absorbing too much UV light and becoming burnt or developing skin cancer.

The more melanin in the skin, the less UV light is absorbed. Skin with more melanin also gives out heat better. These clever melanin skills are helpful where it's hot and sunny. In the same way, in places with less sunshine, less melanin in the skin ensures more UV rays get through so they can produce enough Vitamin D. Human beings most likely all started with darker skin due to living in hotter regions, but as some migrated to places with less sun, their melanin was reduced so they got enough Vitamin D.

Everyone has some melanin – it's what gives human skin its base colour. This means we all have a variation of the same skin colour. Melanin also gives us our different eye and hair colours. The amount of melanin we start with is genetic. When skin is exposed to sunlight, it generates more melanin and so your skin starts to become darker.

Now that you know that everyone has the same brown pigment in their skin, but in different amounts, you might be baffled at the different names given to different skin colours. White and black are the most surprising adjectives because our actual skin colours are quite different. But other even more baffling descriptions include red, yellow and even blue!

KHOUDIA DIOP

Khoudia Diop (1996–) grew up in Senegal. Even though her skin complexion is common there, she was teased for being dark. She says, "I learned to tune out the negativity, which made me more confident and taught me to love myself. Having support from family, friends – and now fans – definitely helps to affirm that I am worthy, loved and beautiful."

Khoudia celebrates her skin colour with the name "The Melanin Goddess" and she says, "All women should feel confident in the skin they're in – everyone is beautiful in their own unique way, and the key is to realise that and celebrate it."

A spectrum of colour

You might be shocked to discover that some people decide how important or valuable someone is depending on how much melanin is in their skin. This is called racism.

Discrimination can happen against all skin colours, or even between people with different shades such as lighter brown and darker brown. This is called colourism or shadeism.

Unfortunately, racism and shadeism have been used in history to exploit and discriminate against people. For example, enslaved Black people were used to enrich the people who kidnapped them. The slavers justified their terrible actions because the people they enslaved had darker skin than them.

Skin comes in all sorts of colours

Today many people are still discriminated against because of their skin colour. This discrimination can range from things like getting paid less or not getting offered a job, or being physically attacked or worse. That's why if we ensure all skin colours are considered equally beautiful, **we're doing something which might seem small, but is incredibly big**. We are correcting historic racism and doing our bit to make a better, more equal, more beautiful future.

The best colour is yours

Throughout history, people have tried to change their skin colour, sometimes to make it lighter and other times to make it darker. The fact they tried these two opposite things goes to show there's no fixed idea about the "best" colour. Because skin is a living, breathing organ, anything done to affect the melanin in it carries significant dangers.

Skin lightening and skin whitening creams contain ingredients to stop melanin from being produced. As we need melanin, this is dangerous. And the ingredients themselves can also be toxic. Creams with hydroquinone cause cancer, and mercury damages your kidneys and brain. Injections or pills of glutathione cause your thyroid and kidneys not to work or can trigger skin rashes and peeling as though it's been burned. Awful!

Tanning triggers your skin to produce more melanin so it looks darker. Tanning from the sun and using sunbeds are both dangerous. Tanning causes genetic damage to the skin and a risk of skin cancer. Some people say a tan looks "healthier" or makes you "glow", but the truth is that sun exposure causes your skin to age prematurely making it look coarse and leathery.

NANDITA DAS

The Indian actor and film director Nandita Das (1969–) has appeared in more than 40 films in ten languages, winning countless awards and honours. Despite her incredible talents, she says she has faced discrimination because of her skin colour.

Nandita is the face of the "India's Got Colour" campaign which challenges the idea that pale skin is the only way to be beautiful. She says, "We don't need to be defining ourselves with the colour of our skin, there is lot more to all of us and we need to explore that… Whatever may be your colour, be comfortable. And let's celebrate our diversity."

SKIN THROUGH HISTORY

It's time to climb back into our time machine to see how ideas about skin have varied through history.

Ancient Egypt (c3000BCE–332CE)

In the streets we hear people raving about how beautiful "golden" skin is and being downright rude about the "reddish brown" skin of poorer men and women who have darker skin because they work outside. Rich people turn their noses up at hard work which is why they think their lighter coloured skin is more beautiful. We don't have any ideas of what is considered beautiful among women who work, which is actually most women. They may have quite different ideas.

Wealthy Egyptian women experiment with make-up. Their preferred look is bold and bright! Crushed jewels like green malachite make brightly coloured make-up, and red ochre is used for lip colour. Black eye liner, which today we call "kohl", creates striking eye make-up and also gives protection from the sun and eye infections caused by desert dust, Nile bacteria and insects.

Bold make-up is fashionable

Ancient Greece (c1200BCE–323BCE)

While women are usually the subjects of beauty, here talk is about how beautiful men are. While eavesdropping on the ancient Greeks, you hear the word "kalos kagathos", which means that if a boy or man is nice to look at, he also has a beautiful mind and personality. What do you make of that?

Aristotle, a famous philosopher, talks about how women are "deformed men". The philosopher Hesiod calls women "kalon kakon" – a "beautiful-evil thing"! He's trying to convince people that women are evil because they are beautiful, and beautiful because they are evil. What strange and horrible ideas! Women are wonderful because they are women. They are not a version of men. And they are definitely not evil. He's right about one thing though – women are all beautiful!

Ancient Rome (753BCE–c500CE)

Skin treatments could get weird in ancient Rome, especially in pursuit of paler skin. Ovid, a famous poet and influential Roman, writes:

RECIPE FOR A WHITENING MIXTURE
Two pounds of barley groats and an equal amount of vetch mix and soften with ten eggs. Then, dry the mixture in the air and grind it in a stone mill driven by a patient donkey. Kill the first horns falling out of the head of a burly stag ($\frac{1}{6}$ a pound). Blow it together in white powder and pour through a sieve. Add twelve peeled narcissus bulbs and knock them together. Finally, add two ounces of gum and Tuscan spelt and nine times more honey. Such a mixture of Romance should be rubbed in the face, to help lighten the complexion effectively.

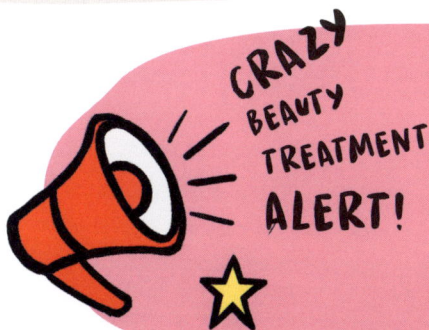

CRAZY BEAUTY TREATMENT ALERT!

Just because a famous influencer said it, doesn't make it good for you. This advice also applies today!

The Middle Ages (5th–late 15th centuries)

Strict beauty rules apply here. Women should be simple and plain in looks and personality. The only pictures of women allowed are from religious stories. Make-up is a no-no because it's said that changing your face is the work of the devil. (Don't worry, it's not. Wanting to feel beautiful is completely normal, whichever era of history you're in!)

If you're considered to be breaking the rules – or even if you're not – you could get labelled a "witch" and suffer gruesome punishments, even death.

The Renaissance (15th century)

Artificial beauty marks are drawn on women's faces to hide scars caused by illnesses like smallpox. Pale skin is in, but the make-up used to create the look contains lead, which burns holes in the skin and can cause death. People stick small fabric patches in different shapes over the resulting holes in their skin.

The Elizabethans (1558–1603)

To copy Queen Elizabeth's pale skin, women use ceruse, which is a mixture of poisonous white lead and vinegar – which ruins their skin. They wash their faces with mercury to reverse the damage. Except mercury is also poisonous and causes you to die slowly.

People put egg whites on their skin believing it will stop wrinkles. Lips are painted bright red with vermillion made from cinnabar, which is a mineral used for paintings. Personally I wouldn't put actual paint on my face!

The Victorians (1837–1901)

Rather strangely, at this time a disease that can kill you is also thought to make you look rather beautiful! Before tuberculosis kills you, it gives your lips and cheeks a blushed look and makes your eyes sparkle.

Other dangerous ways to look beautiful that could also kill you: a splash of mercury on the eyelashes, a few drops of deadly nightshade in the eyes, a dash of ammonia on the face and eating arsenic wafers for translucent skin!

The toilet mask

In 1875, American hatmaker and dressmaker Madame Helen M Rowley invented the "Mask For Medical Purposes" made of flexible rubber. The aim was making the face lightly sweat to soften and clear the skin and fix acne, blotches and pimples. Worn while sleeping, it promised to "beautify, bleach and preserve the complexion."

The 1920s

Immediately you notice that some women look tanned. They are copying famous fashion designer Coco Chanel who came back from holiday sunburned. Remember back in the ancient world where light skin was all the rage? Well, here it's fashionable to have a tan. Which just goes to show how ideas of beauty change.

The Second World War (1939–1945)

Adverts tell women to "keep your beauty on duty" and their role in winning the war is to "look good for Britain." Women are told to get dressed up and look glamorous so men will feel a morale boost and have more energy to fight the war.

It's a very strange idea that "being beautiful" for other people is a job for women, as though that's the only thing they do, or that it is even something that you have to do just because you are a woman! In fact, during the war women do lots of traditionally male jobs. Some even say women keep the country running while the men are away fighting. Being tough, resilient and brave in difficult circumstances and keeping the nation going... now that's beautiful!

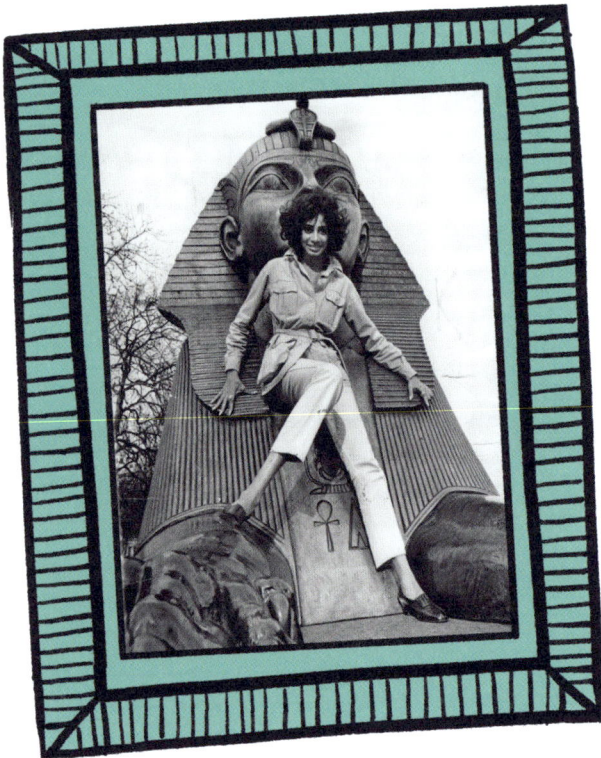

The 1960s and '70s

Changes are happening to celebrate a wider range of beauty ideas, skin colours, hair types and body shapes. A campaign called "Black is Beautiful" encourages people to think about all the different ways to be beautiful. Black truly is beautiful... and so is brown, cream, freckled and every other shade.

In 1966, British *Vogue* has a Black woman on its cover for the first time: Donyale Luna. American *Vogue* follows with Beverly Johnson, but not until 1974.

A perfume called "Charlie" becomes all the rage, and Black woman Darnella Thomas is its spokesperson.

Donyale Luna

Naomi Campbell

The 1980s

This decade sees the emergence of global supermodels, including Naomi Campbell. She says that some countries don't use the adverts she is in because she is Black. Other supermodels like Christy Turlington and Linda Evangelista say, "If you don't use Naomi, you don't get us." They all go on to be famous and successful, which shows how important it is to support each other.

The 1990s

Just before we return to the present, here's one thing that makes us smile: the news that an Indian woman has been named the world's most beautiful woman. In 1994, Aishwarya Rai Bachchan is crowned Miss World.

The 21st century

As we race back home to the 21st century, we see that a popular idea is "contouring" – where make-up is used to make the face look a totally different shape.

Aishwarya Rai Bachchan

New technologies have always been used to change appearance, whether it's special creams, tanning lotions or rubber face masks. Apps, filters and social media are the newest technology used for creating ideas about beauty. Instead of having to be wealthy and employ artists or sculptors, women can now create their own images.

SKINTASTIC

No one has the same skin all over their body – it can vary in texture, stretchiness, thickness and shade. The palms of your hands are different to the concertina-type skin on your knees, for example. And your skin can change moment to moment, if you're hot, cold, scared or blushing.

Albinism and vitiligo, it's a melanin thing

Sometimes there can be notable variation in how melanin is produced in different parts of the skin. Vitiligo is when paler patches occur, often on the face, neck, hands and in skin creases. In albinism, the body produces less melanin and so skin, hair and eyes are very pale. In both cases, extra protection is needed from the sun.

WINNIE HARLOW

Canadian Winnie Harlow (1994–) became a model after a TV competition. Initially she found it hard to deal with her vitiligo, but with the help of her family she began to accept herself. She says, "I try not to compare myself to anyone else... Take my aspiration of being what I want to be and put that in your life to do what you actually, really dream to do."

Unique spots of beauty

Beauty spots are small, dark dots found in all sorts of places on the body and face, and they are a special form of being beautiful. Some people have "birth marks" that sometimes, but not always, fade over time.

"A face without freckles is like a night without stars," so the saying goes. Freckles are little areas where there is more melanin which can appear, disappear or increase with time.

When skin is damaged such as by cuts and burns, it has the amazing ability to repair itself. Emergency skin looks different and we call it a scar. Weirdly, too many stories and films associate scars with villains. When in fact, a scar is actually yet another sign of your superhero skin. **All of these are part of the unique story your skin tells about you.** And loving them is an important part of loving yourself.

MEGHAN MARKLE

The Duchess of Sussex (1981–) loves her freckles and her skin tone. She says, "My pet peeve is when my skin tone is changed and my freckles are airbrushed out of a photoshoot."

Realising that there are many different ways of being beautiful gives her a sense of meaning. She says, "I have the most vivid memories of being seven years old and my mum picking me up from my grandmother's house. There were the three of us, a family tree in an ombré of mocha next to the caramel complexion of my mum and light-skinned, freckled me. I remember the sense of belonging having nothing to do with the colour of my skin."

EM FORD

The award-winning content creator, filmmaker and photographer Em Ford (1990–) shared a video about having acne in 2015, and it gathered 10 million views. Some people left horrid comments, but she ignored them. She says, "It's not you – it's them. If someone is sending or leaving abuse online, they usually have serious issues or problems going on in their life. When I realised this, I started looking at comments in an entirely different way."

She adds, "Beauty should be about how you feel, not how you look. So instead of constantly searching for a product which may make you 'look' a certain way, look for something which can make you feel a certain way... It can be hard to remember the most important thing – you ARE beautiful."

Growing up and growing older

When we are teenagers, our hormones change, which can cause acne. This can be upsetting, but it's a normal part of growing up. Occasionally it takes longer to pass or some people may need medical help, but for most people, keeping your skin clean and using the right products mean it will pass.

As you grow, you might notice stretch marks on your body because the skin expands rapidly. Women can also get them after having babies as the skin around their tummies has to stretch. These marks are phenomenal because they show how you've changed over time. Or that a human being was grown inside someone – just like you were!

Over time, we get wrinkles, crows' feet and laughter lines from using our faces to express joy, happiness, sadness, worry, astonishment, surprise and delight. That's why we love people with interesting faces!

Ageism makes people worry about looking old. But it's not our age that needs to be changed, but our ideas. All skin – young, old, smooth or wrinkled – is beautiful. The sad truth is there's a lot of pressure not to have wrinkles. But to avoid them, you'd have to defy nature and be frozen in time. Which would be no fun. While everyone was living life, you'd just be watching them inside your frozen-in-time ice cube.

Life is for living, whatever your age. Be proud that your skin shows you growing up and living life!

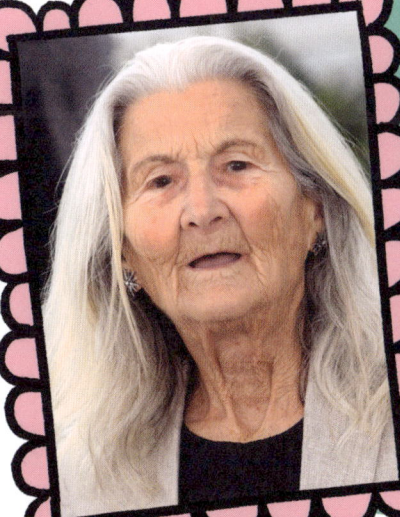

BENEDICTA SANCHEZ

At the age of 84, Benedicta Sánchez (1934–) won the Best New Actress Award in Spain – the oldest woman ever to do so. She had no previous acting experience! Benedicta appeared at the awards ceremony without her teeth: "They were being fixed." She says, "Life hands you surprises, and this is a very big one in my long existence."

Changing your skin

Your skin can be an amazing canvas for you to try out different ways to express yourself. Some methods can be like creating art, BUT others can be harmful and permanently damaging. So choose carefully!

Make-up can quickly change your look to keep up with the latest styles or present a different image of yourself. Perhaps something from the history section inspires you? The point of make-up should not be to look identical to everyone else; it's to show your individuality.

Concealers and foundation cover up blemishes, skin tone variations, freckles and scars. Anti-ageing creams claim to reduce wrinkles. But as we are learning in this chapter, all these kinds of skin are normal, so we shouldn't feel bad about them.

Tattoos change your skin permanently by injecting ink under the skin. You need to be 18 before having a tattoo because it carries risks. In the meantime, try out henna or glitter tattoos which are lots of fun, safe and easily removed.

Botox and dermal fillers are injected into the skin to paralyse the muscles so they don't move or to plump up the skin like padding. It's done because people don't want wrinkles like the ones that appear when you smile. But then you'd be smiling with your eyes and no one would know.

Apps and filters can be fun for making silly faces and adding stories to your images. But you should be careful not to alter how your actual face appears. It might seem harmless, but it can be quite dangerous for your mental health and self-esteem. Find out more on page 105.

It's true that these surface treatments can give us a boost and make us feel good inside. And that's fine. Just make sure you're not using them to hide your unhappiness or change yourself for others. And keep a special watch out for dangerous chemicals or toxic ingredients.

The important thing is to check you are not changing the outside as a way of fitting in, or covering up unhappiness on the inside. Or to make other people happy (other people will never be happy).

Remember: the power of how you express yourself through your skin is to be more of who you are, not less.

CLEOPATRA

Cleopatra (c69BCE–30BCE) was a clever politician who turned Egypt into the most powerful region under Rome and married two of its leaders, Julius Caesar and Mark Anthony. She spoke many languages and was known for being very charming. She raised an army and led a naval fleet into battle.

Legend says she was very beautiful because some people think the only way a woman can be powerful is to be beautiful. Others say she was ugly and looked like a man. Either way, Cleopatra didn't care what other people thought of her.

She probably had brown skin as she was of Egyptian heritage. Her trademark look was her green eyeshadow and striking kohl eyeliner. She's probably the first woman whose make-up is part of her story, and even in depictions of her today, her bold look is constantly reinvented. This image is a sculpture created out of scrap metal in 2020.

How to be skintastic

The most beautiful skin is the one that's loved, healthy and properly looked after rather than having anything to do with a particular colour, freckle, wrinkle or spot. Respect and celebrate your skin and that of other people. Encourage others to be comfortable in theirs. Don't be the grinch that makes comments about other people's skin – because all that means is that you are not confident in your own.

People "glow" because they're happy on the inside with who they are – that's the whole idea of inner beauty! If you're beautiful on the inside it literally shines out of you!

Even on days when you're feeling a bit wobbly inside, your skin is always there for you, keeping you all together in one place. In fact, right now, say a little "thank you" to your brilliant skin. Or find someone you love and touch your skin to theirs. Maybe you'll feel a tickle or a tingle or a spark of love with them.

GEMMA CHAN

The highly acclaimed actor and UNICEF ambassador (1982–) had doubts about herself growing up. She says, "I had very awkward teenage years. I tried a bit of everything, as you do when you're a teenager and you don't know what your style is yet. I definitely didn't feel like I was attractive…"

About getting older, she says, "Every wrinkle, everything on your face is an embodiment and an expression of the life that you've lived. The more you laugh, the more wrinkles you have… The most important part of being beautiful is balance… I love beauty. I love products. I love fashion. And it's all great fun, but I think looking after what's on the inside is as important."

Support your skin's superhero powers. Keep your skin:

CLEAN – Regular washing and cleaning will keep skin healthy, reduce bacteria and limit problems like acne and pimples.

MOISTURISED – Helping skin stay soft will make it look and feel good.

HYDRATED – Dry skin can't do its job properly and it loses its lustre so drink plenty of water.

LOVED – If you're happy on the inside, your skin will glow on the outside.

OBSERVED – Keep an eye out for anything unusual like inflammation or injury, which sometimes can affect darker skin without anyone noticing. Watch out for skin conditions like eczema or changes in skin pigmentation like beauty spots that appear and then get bigger.

Be good to your skin. You'll wear it every day for the rest of your life.

EMBRACE MANY WAYS TO BE BEAUTIFUL

Let's jump in a jet and travel around the world to see what ideas about beauty exist in different places and cultures. What do you think we might find? You're a very clued-up detective now, so you can probably already guess that the BIG DISCOVERY is that people have different ideas about what it means to be beautiful. Just as ideas about beauty have changed through history, other countries, heritages and cultures have different ideas about beauty, too. Around the world, and even in the places we live and the communities we are part of, we can find so many gorgeous looks, body shapes, hairstyles and skin colours. And we know why: because there is no single fixed way of being beautiful!

BEAUTY AROUND THE WORLD

If you've been paying careful attention, you will have noticed this: what other cultures think is beautiful can be different to what we think is beautiful, and what we find beautiful might not be the case for other cultures. That's not because one way of being beautiful is better than another, but in fact the opposite: each culture has its own ideas of what is beautiful, and their ideas are as beautiful to them as our ideas are to us.

No single idea

Some artists have been exploring what beauty means around the world. Natalia Ivanova is a photographer who captures images of people who are considered beautiful in their own culture in a project called Les Origines de la Beauté (The Origins of Beauty). The final montage she has created is a stunning image of how much beauty there is in the world. What jumps out is how very many different ways there are to be beautiful.

Each of the photos that make up the large image on the previous page is just one single snapshot, based on one person in that culture. Each culture changes over time and has different ideas within it, too. The image also doesn't show all the cultures in the world now, let alone since the beginning of time. And none of these pictures show all the gorgeous ways that age, ability, skin texture (you know the long list by now) vary how people look. I wish I could show you all of them, but there is one place you can see and enjoy them – in the world!

NIMMI

In 1952, you see a poster for a Bollywood movie originally called *Aan*, but given the English title *The Savage Princess*. It's the first film from India to be shown in UK cinemas and stars Bollywood actor Nimmi (1933–2020), who is a famous Indian film star and beauty icon.

When Hollywood star Errol Flynn – one of the most famous celebrities in the world at the time – tries to kiss Nimmi's hand, she pulls it away and the newspapers call her "the unkissed girl of India". Later she tells reporters that, "He asked permission to tickle my toes. I said no." Nimmi knew she was the owner of her own body. If she didn't want to be touched, even by a celebrity, that was up to her. Part of being beautiful is owning your beauty and standing up for yourself.

It sounds strange to say it, but in Britain at the time, they might never have thought of women from India as beautiful, let alone as glamorous film stars!

The same humans but different looks

You might look at the ideas of beauty in this chapter and raise an eyebrow and think, really? But remember, other cultures might – and in fact do! – think exactly the same about you and your culture, too. When opinionated people say that this or that is the right way to be beautiful, that is what is called a culture's **beauty ideals** (see page 98 to learn more).

Some people go on and on so much about their version of beauty being the only one that is right that it can feel like your brain is going to explode. Ignore them: you know in your heart that in different cultures there are different looks which are just as beautiful as yours.

So, why DO ideas about beauty vary in different cultures?

Tick which of these you think is the answer:

Their body shapes, hair and skin are different to yours. ☐

They live in a different part of the world, where things like the environment, the weather and the work they do are different to yours. ☐

They have their own history, traditions and culture and so their ideas have developed differently. ☐

They have different ideas about the roles of women in their culture, and therefore different beauty ideals for women. ☐

Okay, smarty-pants! You knew that was a trick question because the answer is ALL of them. There are lots of reasons why ideas about beauty vary in different cultures, just as ideas about beauty are changing constantly in your own history and culture.

FINDING JOY IN EACH OTHER'S BEAUTY

Have you ever borrowed an item of clothing or some make-up from a friend because when they wore it you really liked the way they looked? Well, cultures do the same with ideas. In all cultures there are lots of ways to be beautiful. This book has limited space so we can't feature all of them but if something here grabs your interest, or a particular culture is relevant to you, go and investigate more!

Henna

The history of henna goes back thousands of years in the Indian subcontinent, Africa and the Middle East. Henna leaves are dried, crushed into a powder and mixed into a paste which is then applied to parts of the body like hands, feet and hair. When removed, it leaves behind a colour anywhere from a pale orange to a deep brown. It cools the skin and can be used to paint beautiful artwork. Many women apply it, especially when they get married.

When I was growing up in Britain, henna was considered very strange, and I would hide my hands when I'd had them decorated at someone's wedding. My teacher would tell me off, and kids would say I was dirty. It was very painful to be told this.

But today, something that was considered beautiful in my culture has been shared. It feels good sharing something beautiful, and it feels even better when the culture that has taken it appreciates its beauty.

Not cool

What if you created a cool beauty trend, but your neighbours said you looked ugly? Then, you're out one day and you see them showing off the look you created and bragging about how beautiful and stylish they are! You'd feel upset, and rightly so! Unfortunately, this happens with ideas about beauty through a process called "cultural appropriation".

Borrowing and adding to ideas is part of how human societies develop and grow through exchange. However, if one culture takes an idea about beauty or style, claims they invented it and look amazing AND AT THE SAME TIME says to the people who created it that they are ugly, then that is a very UGLY thing to do.

It is important to acknowledge where an idea about beauty came from and to respect those who created the idea and their traditions.

Sharing not comparing

Sharing ideas about what it means to be beautiful is WONDERFUL and it reminds us that there is no one fixed idea. Everyone can keep experimenting with their own style and self-expression, as well as learning new things. However, comparing ideas about beauty to suggest one culture is better than another one is NOT WONDERFUL.

Sometimes a culture uses its beauty ideals to make another group feel bad about itself, as though their own looks are a reason they are superior. (Earlier in the book we talked about racism and colourism.) This is bullying and, of course, is just plain wrong. The sad part is that, by behaving this way, they are slowly getting uglier on the inside. And you know what I'm going to say: ugliness on the inside definitely ends up showing on the outside in the end.

DANGEROUS BEAUTY IDEALS

Many cultures, including our own, have dangerous ideas about beauty. Here are four ideas from four different cultures which are largely moving into the past, but they are a good reminder of how beauty ideals change, how all cultures including our own have dangerous ideas and that putting our health before any kind of idea of beauty is so important! It can be hard to spot dangerous beauty ideals in our own culture, so thinking about others and then reflecting on our own is a good way to do that.

Scarification

This is a skin technique dating back to the early days of human history, which is popular in many parts of Africa, as well as among aboriginal Australians and in places like Papua New Guinea. The skin is cut in different designs so when it heals back, the scars form a pattern that stands out. The patterns can be a sign of reaching adulthood or to show which tribe someone belongs to, and they are considered a sign of beauty.

DON'T TRY THIS! Scarification carries risks like bleeding, infection or not healing correctly. It is slowly fading in popularity.

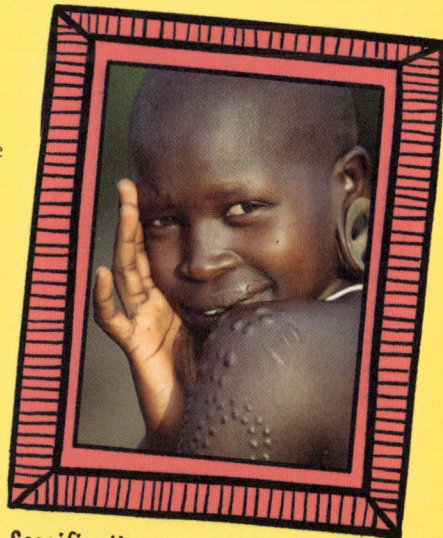

Scarification causes raised patterns on the skin

Something to think about: Just like scarification, tattoos can be considered a form of self-expression. However, it is important to remember that, just like scarification, if not done safely they carry a risk of scarring, infection and even poisoning. And they're permanent.

Leblouh

In traditional Mauritanian culture, the bigger the woman, the more beautiful she was considered to be. Women were forced to eat large amounts of food (leblouh) so they put on weight and therefore become more popular for marriage. Today, modern medicines are sometimes used for women to gain weight, but these also have dangerous health risks.

Something to think about: Doing unhealthy and dangerous things to become bigger is just as wrong as doing unhealthy and dangerous things to become thinner, such as extreme dieting, taking weight-loss pills or forcing your body into tight corsets.

Foot binding

For over a thousand years in China, breaking and tightly binding young girls' feet resulted in small feet which were considered attractive for women. Such tiny, damaged feet were painful and meant that women couldn't walk properly – so it supposedly showed that they were so rich they didn't need to walk or work. It was also a sign of belonging to a particular ethnic group, in this case the Han Chinese. It was made illegal in 1912.

Feet that were bound

Something to think about: Everyone likes to show that they belong to a tribe or a group (although no one group is better than another). But sometimes these ways of showing belonging involve permanently changing your body – often through pressure. Think about the example of foot binding. When it comes to feet, are ideas much different today? Women may wear stilettos or very high heels because it makes them look taller and their legs look longer. But they risk ankle injuries, arthritis and long-term back problems.

Tapeworm diet

Remember – people in the Western world have strange and dangerous ideas about beauty, too. To become as thin as possible, women in the Victorian era were encouraged to ingest tapeworm eggs. Once inside the woman's intestines, the tapeworm would grow (up to 20 metres!) and consume a good portion of the food she was eating. Being thin and looking a bit ill were the beauty ideals of the time.

Something to think about: Unfortunately, some people still try this even today in places like the UK, USA and Hong Kong. The side effects can be fatal. I don't know about you, but just thinking about it gives me the creeps. Thank goodness it's illegal. Don't do it, kids!

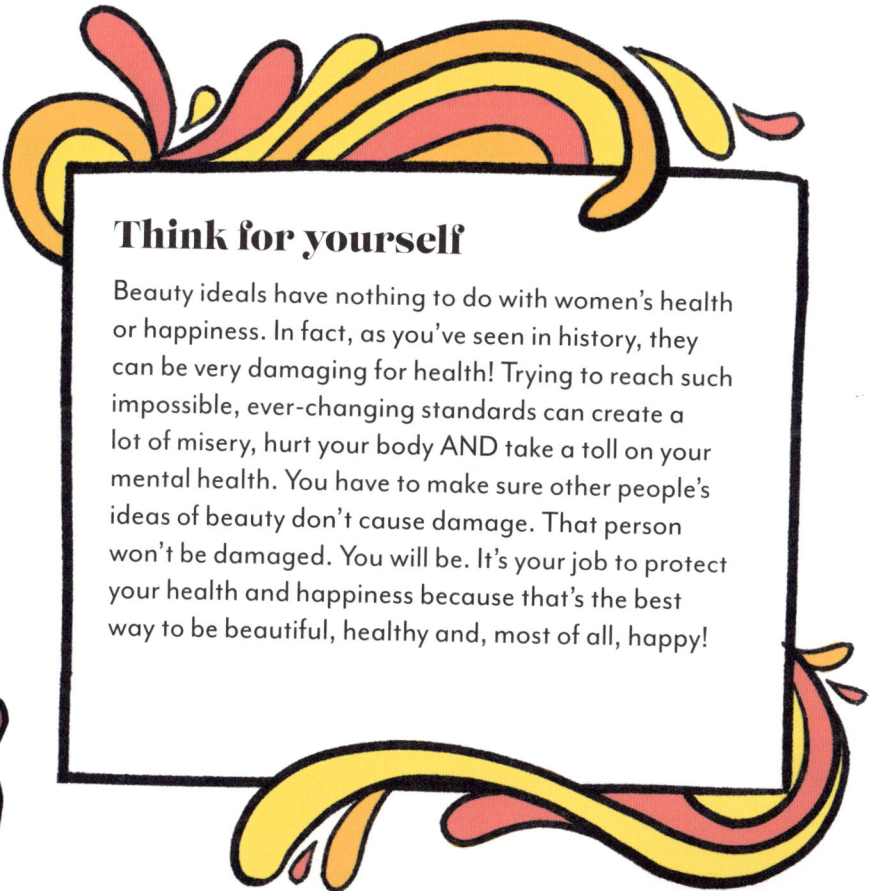

Think for yourself

Beauty ideals have nothing to do with women's health or happiness. In fact, as you've seen in history, they can be very damaging for health! Trying to reach such impossible, ever-changing standards can create a lot of misery, hurt your body AND take a toll on your mental health. You have to make sure other people's ideas of beauty don't cause damage. That person won't be damaged. You will be. It's your job to protect your health and happiness because that's the best way to be beautiful, healthy and, most of all, happy!

THE ONE AND ONLY YOU

Can you imagine anything worse than everyone in the whole world looking identical? It would be dull, and you'd get mixed up with other people. In lessons, the teacher wouldn't be able to tell who's who. And pictures from your birthday party would look like only one person had been there and they'd been photoshopped into the picture loads of times. The point is, the very fact that there are lots of ways to be beautiful is itself beautiful. If you want a grand phrase to describe this, then you can say diversity IS beauty.

YOU-ness

Let's think about all the different things that can be combined to create a look. There's body shape, size, height, skin colour, body parts and ability. There's hair colour, texture, length and style. There are different kinds of facial features. Then there's style, fashion and attitude. Just think about how many different combinations you can have! There are billions and billions. And of all these billions of combinations, there is only ONE beautiful, gorgeous, unique YOU.

Here's a tongue twister for you: **the brilliant breath-taking beauty of beauty is the different diverse divine distinct delightful dramatic wonderful wicked ways to be brilliantly beautiful.**

"Everyone is kneaded out of the same dough, but not baked in the same oven."

YIDDISH PROVERB

A boring world

If there was only one way to be beautiful, just like all the bossy people say, just imagine what it would be like. This book would only be one page long, with just one picture of one person, who might look like a LEGO person. It would not have much to say: "Being square is good because it's the only way you can be. Make sure your hair can come off and on and be put on backwards, if necessary. And your skin colour must be extremely bright yellow. THE END."

While that book would have been much less work for me to write (and much, much quicker for you to read), it would have been BOOOOOORING. You wouldn't have explored all the beautiful and interesting ways to be a unique human being, and you wouldn't have enjoyed all the gorgeous looks, styles and ideas from history and from around the world that you've seen.

Your story

You should feel excited about your own individual kind of beauty and all the things you do to present yourself because this tells the story of who you are. It tells the world about your heritage: it says something about your family and background. You can use your body to show you support a particular idea, such as a protest movement. Or you can show other things you want people to know about you. That's like me and my headscarf. I wear it for lots of reasons, and one of them is to tell people that I'm Muslim.

Of course, some people like to show more of these things, and others like to express less about themselves. And that in itself shows our diversity. Either way, whether it's little or big glimpses that you show of yourself to the world, all of them are things to be proud of.

Your history

You should also feel proud of all the bits of you that look like they do, because they all say a little bit about your history. Sometimes parts of you look like your parents. Sometimes you don't look like your parents because the likenesses skipped a generation. You might look like other relatives instead, or you might be adopted and have different DNA. And that's also part of who you are. Because whether you look similar to, or completely and utterly different from, your family, everything inside you – your history, culture, ideas and self-expression – comes together as a beautiful blend and creates something unique.

Sometimes more than one heritage can come together in a single person because they might have parents and family from different origins. While you are trying to figure out your own idea of being beautiful, you might feel like you're not quite the beauty ideal of one culture or another. But the important thing to remember is that everyone has something about them that's a bit different. I always tell myself that instead of feeling awkward, being different, being my Unique-Me™ is actually my superpower. Because that little bit of being different is about my own unique personality and my own way of being beautiful.

Unique-Me™ is a trademark for knowing that all the different bits of you come together to make up the single individual that you are. No one else can be you. Getting a Unique-Me trademark is all about being happy in who you are. If you had to describe your trademark you, what qualities and descriptions would it include?

Finding your place

Some people belong to more than one group because their parents, families or the place they live have a mix of different cultures and heritages. That can feel exciting but also confusing. To untangle it, the best way is to learn about the ideas of beauty in each culture, and then find your own place in it, remembering that you are you, that everyone is beautiful and that thinking you are beautiful is the most beautiful thing. It is also important to remember, as you've already learnt, that cultures, heritages and ideas all keep changing, and often the good changes happen because of people who are happy and proud to be different, and are confident in their difference.

I am Indian, and also African, and also British, and also I choose to wear a headscarf because I'm Muslim. I love all the different kinds of ideas of beauty in each of those cultures. I love how the mix of them makes me who I am and makes up the way I look. I can be similar but also just a bit different, too, which all adds up to me being myself.

CELEBRATE DIFFERENCE

Being excited about diversity in beauty is such a brilliant thing that you can SHOUT IT FROM THE ROOFTOPS. Okay, not literally. But you can nudge the person next to you and say, "Hey! It's brilliant that everybody looks different because they get to be them, and you get to be you, and I get to be me." What is particularly beautiful is that if you help others to realise that they are beautiful, then that makes the world a better place.

Activism

Sometimes people feel like they need to make really big changes to the world, like stopping climate change or ending poverty. Or making sure children never have to eat Brussels sprouts again. (I know all the parents reading that line are glaring at me now.) And it is important to work hard to make the world better. That's called being an activist.

Making yourself feel happy in your skin, making other people feel good about themselves and respecting and appreciating that everyone around the world is just as beautiful as each other might sound like a small thing compared to those huge issues. But it's not. It's huge. Because being happy about yourself, feeling positive and pushing yourself forward instead of holding yourself back can unleash you as a force for good in the world. **It's not a small thing to believe you are beautiful and you are your unique YOU: believing that everyone is beautiful instead of listening to all the negative ideas in the world might be one of the most activist things of all.**

The science bit

It's strange that people like to point out how different people are, when human beings are mostly all the same. Correction, more than 99.9% of a human being is the same as everyone else. Only one teeny tiny part, 0.1% of your genes, is different from other people. (Genes are the information that determines how your body works and looks.)

So when someone says that people are very different, there is something quick and brainy you can reply: "We're not so different: actually, nearly all of us is the same. And the teeny tiny bit that is actually different means everyone can be their own unique self so that we are not all boringly identical!"

Over the long history of human beings, our genes have slowly adapted to our environments. These changes explain why we are different colours, sizes and shapes. Otherwise, we might all just be simple one-celled bacteria. And then this book would be even shorter than the one-page LEGO person book. It would just be a drawing of a blob with the words "All blobs are beautiful". Not that there's anything wrong with being a blob, of course. But I'm glad to be a human, and thrilled that we have so many different ways to be beautiful. Aren't you?

One of a kind

The part of us that makes us different is pretty important. In fact, we are so unique that one study suggests that the chances of finding just one pair of people with the same size and spacing of facial features among all the 7.4 billion people on the planet is only one in 135! But even if you did find someone who looks like you, they still wouldn't be you! That's the case even for identical twins. They wouldn't have your style, your fashion or your self-expression. But most importantly, they wouldn't have your brain or your personality – which are all key bits of your beauty. Because your inner beauty and your personality – the attitudes and facial expressions and how you hold your body – all affect the way you look! Which means there's only one actual you. So why not celebrate it?

"What you love is always beautiful."

FRENCH PROVERB

"Beauty is ten, nine of which is dressing."

AZERBAIJANI PROVERB

"Beauty is not in the face; beauty is a light in the heart."

KHALIL GIBRAN,
LEBANESE AMERICAN WRITER, POET AND ARTIST

"Good health is the sister of beauty."

MALTESE PROVERB

"A beautiful thing is never perfect."

EGYPTIAN PROVERB

"Everything has beauty, but not everyone sees it."

CONFUCIUS, CHINA

"Beauty never travels in a group."

ARABIAN PROVERB

"A good character is real beauty that never fades."

BURMESE PROVERB

BE THE BOSS OF YOUR OWN BEAUTY

As a clever global beauty detective, you have spotted that ideas about beauty vary through history and by culture. But have you ever asked yourself: **Why** do ideas about beauty vary? And **how** are beauty ideals created? **Who** decides what is beautiful and how do they make us agree with them? And are we even looking at what we think we're looking at?

WHAT IS BEAUTY?

Yaeba

Some scientists think beauty can be measured in experiments, but this can't be the whole story. It can't explain why we might think our mum or child is the most beautiful person in the world (mine is!) or why in Japan some women think making their teeth crooked and uneven on purpose is more attractive. (This is a process called "yaeba".) Science doesn't explain why Queen Elizabeth I's red hair was copied by all the women of the Royal court or why they made their teeth look rotten like hers!

Can maths decide who is beautiful?

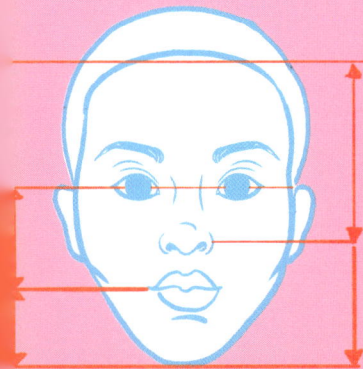

In ancient Greece, mathematicians wanted to find a mathematical answer to everything, including the question, "What makes a person beautiful?" The mathematician Pythagoras (who you might recognise from maths at school) said there is a "golden ratio" you can use to measure how beautiful a person is. He said that a "beautiful" woman's face should be two thirds as wide as it is long, and both sides of the face should be perfectly symmetrical. Was he right? Let's shout it out: "We know that there are so many different ways to be beautiful and you can't make up rules about it or measure it." Phew, **that felt good!**

Unconventional beauty

Science and maths definitely can't explain the idea of being an "unconventional beauty". These are grown-up fancy words to mean, "We thought that there were strict rules for what is beautiful, but it turns out there aren't. All sorts of people are beautiful, who knew?!"

It's someone who doesn't necessarily follow the golden ratio, who isn't perfect and might not be symmetrical. It's someone who you just kind of know is beautiful because of their style, how they hold themselves, the fact that they're imperfect in their beauty (according to the "rules" but who gets to decide the rules anyway?) and because they are specifically not like everyone else.

BARBRA STREISAND

Barbra Streisand (1942–) is an American Jewish singer, actor and filmmaker. Barbra was bullied at school for the shape of her nose, and casting directors rejected her for being "talented but too ugly". Nevertheless, she refused to have plastic surgery. Instead, Barbra did her own thing. She used her looks to play a range of characters from the very serious to the vulnerable, to the extremely comic. In the opening scene of her first, and possibly most famous film, *Funny Girl*, she walks up to a mirror and says, "Hello, gorgeous," and immediately changes everyone's idea of beauty.

You can try it now, too: look in a mirror, just like Barbra Streisand, and tell yourself, "Hello, gorgeous."

Where do beauty ideals come from?

So, we've seen that science alone can't explain why some kinds of looks are preferred over others. Sometimes, in the past, being rich was the important thing: if you looked rich, you were considered more attractive. Which of course is nothing to do with actually being beautiful and everything to do with money.

The role of women

Each society decides the role it thinks that women are supposed to fulfil within it, and therefore how women should look so they can achieve this role. Beauty therefore becomes a way to express what's important in that society at that time. Maybe it's to do with how the ruler looks – like with Elizabeth I. Maybe, like in the Victorian era, it is to be as perfect and angelic as possible, and so the look is to be natural and make-up free. In some societies, beauty ideals represent the powerful people within that society. So women that are described as beautiful represent the ruling classes, but people who look different are seen as inferior. Which is of course completely wrong and also incorrect.

For example, during slavery in the USA, when white people enslaved Black people, white skin was considered more beautiful than Black skin. White people at that time thought there was something better about their skin that made them better human beings. You know that all skin colours are as beautiful as each other, and all human beings are equal. It is the quality of your character and inner beauty that makes you stand out.

Or take the example of the Suffragettes, who fought for women's rights, especially the right to vote. People constantly called them ugly – which those who didn't want women to have rights thought was the worst insult a woman could be given. Those opponents of women's rights thought that the most important thing about a woman was her looks.

Suffragettes campaigning for the right to vote

Voices in the media

Beauty ideals become accepted when we see them over and over again, particularly when famous or influential people try to live up to them. If all the women in a magazine look similar, then that makes us think that that look is the ideal, even if that's not how all the different beautiful women around us in real life look. However, if we're surrounded by all sorts of different images of women, then we can see that there are all sorts of ways to look beautiful. This is called representation.

Your superhero power

Beauty ideals are very powerful because for so long women have been told that their most important quality is how they look. Today women have so many more rights, talents, goals and hopes for their futures. Anyone who thinks that any human being – man or woman – is worth something because of how they look, or gives them better or worse treatment because of their looks, needs to be looked at (did you like my pun?). And that's why just KNOWING that there are lots of ways to be beautiful is POWERFUL. You're busy making history! That makes you a SUPERHERO!

THE IMAGES ALL AROUND US

You can feel pressure to look a certain way because of all the images that surround you. Your brain starts to think that this is how a woman is supposed to look and that if you look like that then it's the only way to be happy. But of course you are too smart to fall for that. You know that happiness comes from the inside. Nevertheless, you have to always be vigilant to avoid falling into the trap of thinking you have to look a particular way. Which means you have to work hard to train your brain that they are not real life. That's important but not easy.

Behind the scenes

One big secret to be busted is that all those women and girls that we see on television, on social media or in magazines that everyone says are beautiful – they don't always look like that in real life! As part of my work, I get to look at what goes on behind the scenes. So, come with me as we sneak behind the camera to see how "beauty" ideals are made. Can you really believe what you see? Is it real? Or is it Fake News?

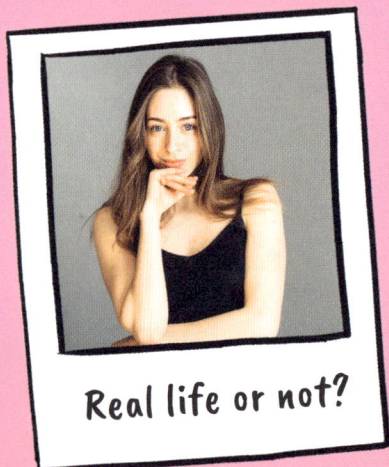

Real life or not?

Creating images

You might be surprised at how many people, how much time and how many different techniques and resources are used to create what look like seemingly ordinary images. A lot of work goes into an image before it looks "natural".

HOW TO GUIDE:

There's a huge process behind getting a simple image in an advert, in a magazine or on a poster.

Behind the scenes

1. Someone (or a group of people) select the look they want to show. A model is chosen from long lists of different models.

2. Specialist fashion stylists choose the clothes and make-up for the desired look.

3. Professional make-up artists and hairdressers create the look.

4. Expert lighting technicians use expensive lights to create the right effect.

5. Props like wind machines are used to capture a pose. Sometimes this can involve getting into dangerous positions.

6. A photographer takes lots and lots and lots of photos. The best one is chosen out of all squillion photos taken.

7. Once the photo is selected, it goes into post-production. This long process uses computer software to edit what the person looks like and their surroundings. It can change their skin colour, body shape, facial expression, body proportions, smoothness of skin, hair... basically anything and everything.

8. Ta dah! At last, a final image.

Manipulating images

There are videos online that demonstrate how images are often manipulated. One famous video starts by showing how the model actually looked to start with (she's already gorgeous), and then it reveals the many steps taken to completely change her look: her eyes are made bigger, her hair is changed, her skin is evened out and its colour changed. Then her body is made thinner, her legs longer and her neck longer. The end result ("beautiful") is completely different from the original person.

Before and after - a model photoshopped

So, we've seen how images can be manipulated beyond recognition to promote unrealistic beauty ideals, but why do people feed us these images? And why do so many people put so much effort into creating these particular images?

Advertising

Advertisers want us to buy their products, so in old-fashioned advertising the theory was that if the people in their adverts look happy, beautiful and fun, then we are attracted to buying those things because we hope it will make us like the people in the adverts. Sometimes those adverts deliberately set out to make us feel bad or guilty so we would buy their products to feel better. They sometimes even said awful things about needing to make ourselves look different – younger, perhaps, or with a different skin colour.

Until recently, adverts weren't very representative – not showing different kinds of people, backgrounds and looks. Thankfully, the advertising industry is changing to be more authentic, representative and inclusive, and to reflect the reality of our lives and all the many ways we really are already beautiful! It's an important step, and good inspiration for all of us.

BUY THIS BOTTLE AND FEEL HAPPY, LIKE ME!

Often adverts promise things to make you feel better... but they don't deliver

Fashion and beauty industries

Fashion and beauty are part of our self-expression, and people like to re-invent their look. The fashion and beauty industries also keep changing the "in" look. Some people say this is to make us think the latest style is the best one so that we keep buying new clothes and make-up. So big hair can mean lots of hairspray. Or having lots of neon eyeshadow as the ideal means spending money on new make-up. Experimenting with new looks is an important part of human life, but what we need to watch out for is any pressure we might feel like we have to constantly change! When we see an advert or a fashion magazine or a beauty image, we just need to add a little asterisk * and in our minds add the words: "it's okay to experiment and keep changing your look, and it's okay just to find the thing you want to be, and just stick with that!"

Something to think about: if everything we see is fantasy and we spend all our time looking at screens and images, and people around us trying to look like that, how can we know what someone really looks like? How do we make sure we see all different kinds of being beautiful?

SOCIAL MEDIA

⭐ So images in adverts and magazines are carefully created, but social media is real people taking real photos, right? Well, sort of. Social media influencers are real people, but they don't always show reality either. Sometimes they hire people to help them photograph posed shots to look "natural", and they can spend huge amounts of time and money to do so.

Social media influencers

Social media influencers select only one photo from many – and post one that they think is most exciting and that will attract the most "likes". They can spend hours editing the photo and the caption before posting it. And they don't always show you the whole of their "real life" – how they look first thing in the morning with crazy bed hair, for example. They don't always tell you what they feel inside, about their own body image, or the problems they are having. And you can be sure that all of those things are definitely happening to them!

Because you don't see behind the scenes of an influencer's life, your brain tricks you and this can leave you feeling sad and thinking, "if only I was like that...". And the worst part is, even lots of influencers say they feel unhappy inside because they feel like their own lives don't match up to their photos. So not only are they affecting other people with their unreal images – they're even affecting themselves. Plus, many influencers feel they have to do ever more crazy or "perfect" things to keep getting "likes". People have borrowed money they can't afford, had terrible accidents and some have even died.

Changing how you look and feel

Of course, not everyone who posts on social media is an "influencer". All of us "normal" people, including your friends and family, might do it, too. However, it can still be tempting to edit how your life appears. There are apps that can change the appearance of your body shape, size, skin colour, facial expression and so on. They claim to "tune" you to be more "beautiful".

While playing around with different looks can be fun, it's important not to keep posting photos that have been tuned or edited. When other people see the fake images it can affect their body image, and none of us should want to make other people feel bad, even if we don't mean to. Seeing your own altered images can negatively change the way you feel about yourself, too. How strange to feel bad comparing yourself to yourself!

The "natural" shot

What it takes to get there

It's not all bad!

Following social media isn't bad – it can be great! As long as we are taking notice of the right images and following people who are out there doing interesting things. Social media is a chance to follow people who look completely different to us, do lots of adventurous and even unfamiliar things and come from other places.

It's good when people do #NoFilter or show other kinds of beauty such as age, different body types or all the many different ways to be beautiful that magazines, TV and other places don't always show you. Be part of their gang and celebrate them and yourself!

BODY IMAGE

Your body image is the collection of thoughts and feelings you have about your body and the way it looks, and how you think it is perceived by others. Your body image isn't connected to how you look on the outside, it's all about how you feel on the inside. You can ask yourself, when you look in a mirror or think about yourself, what do you feel?

Body image and media

Your attitude towards your body – and other people's bodies – is shaped by your community, your family, your culture and yourself. Television shows, movies, music and advertising are all part of popular culture, and what you see, hear and experience all has an effect on how you perceive your body, to greater or lesser degrees, depending on the individual. Some people say that staged, air-brushed images are a kind of "art". Art is an important part of human life. Sometimes people want to create glamorous pictures, or escapism, or fantasy, and that's okay. However, it's important to remember that images still affect how we feel and what we think is "normal" and "natural" for someone to look like.

Why does it matter?

If someone has a positive body image (hurrah!), they generally think YAY! My body is okay. But some people develop a negative body image. You'll probably love some bits of you more than others. That's normal. But what's important is feeling good about yourself overall. As you grow up, your body will be changing, so it's to be expected for your feelings about your body to change.

Your body image and self-esteem (how you feel about yourself) affect your mental health. And this affects your actions, such as what you decide to do or not do. And that has an impact on your physical health, as well as all the fun things we can do in our lives. People with a stronger body image do better in their schoolwork, get more involved in fun activities, go out and about more and are generally happier.

Take control!

Only when you realise that the pictures you see have been edited can you and your brain start to relax. You can rest assured that you're not going crazy wondering how to look like those pictures! There are just a lot of impossible-to-live-up-to pictures. So the best way to have a positive body image is to make sure what goes into your brain is true and accurate. YOU control your body image and you can work on strengthening it. You can talk to grown-ups and teachers, you can chat to your friends, you can read books like this one. And luckily they have lots of helpful tips. The main thing is to want to feel positive, and to help you there are people and ideas everywhere on how to do so.

Body dysmorphia

A serious paragraph now. Sometimes, your body image is affected so negatively that it can turn into an illness. It doesn't mean you are a bad person. It just means you need help. Body dysmorphia is when a person's idea about their body is completely different to how it actually is. They become obsessed with it, often doing unhealthy or even dangerous things to change the way it looks. Eating disorders are when people eat in an irregular way to try and change their body. These include things you might have heard of like anorexia and bulimia. Poor body image can also lead to mental health illnesses like depression and anxiety. If you're worried about any of these in yourself or someone you know, speak to a grown-up.

Speak up!

Lots of celebrities say they don't even recognise heavily edited images of themselves, and this can cause them to feel bad about the way they look in real life. Or they say, "I look great in real life!" and they are offended that the people creating the images change how they look, as though there was something wrong with them. Some celebrities have publicly said that changing images is nonsense. And if they can do it, you can do it, too!

JAMEELA JAMIL

Jameela Jamil (1986–) is an actor, radio presenter, writer, model and activist. She says that seeing fake images when she was younger led to her anorexia. As someone in the public eye, she's had many pictures taken of her, and she's been upset and angry when they've been airbrushed. Her thought was: "How dare they?"

She says, "'Perfect' imagery in magazines hurt me as a teenager, and made sure I never felt good enough [...] We need to see spots. We need to see wrinkles. We need to see cellulite and stretch marks [...] We all have these things on our own bodies. I'm comfortable, I enjoy my body."

Jameela says that we should shout about all the amazing achievements we have in our lives instead of worrying about what silly things people say about how we look.

Try this

Stare at the cross on the left-hand coloured image for around 30 seconds without moving your eyes. Then move your eyes to the cross on the right-hand side. What do you see? What happens is that, even though the circles on the right are white, your eyes see an after-effect of the reverse of the colours in the coloured circles. Because red and green are opposite colours, their positions swap, as do the positions of the blue and yellow circles.

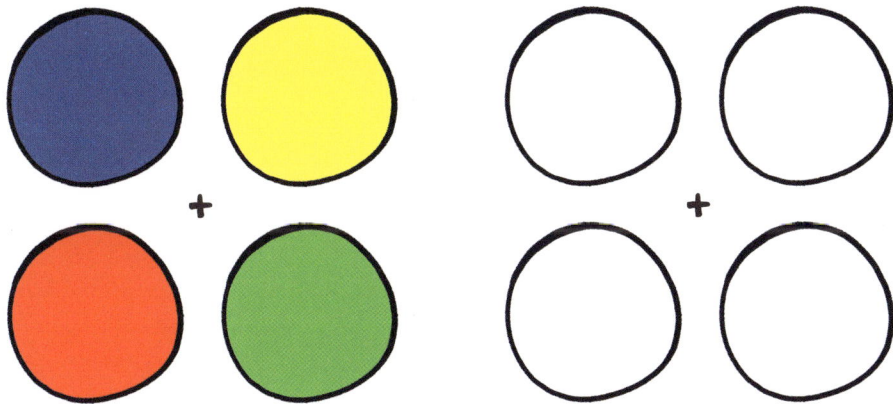

Staring at the coloured circles changes how you see the white circles: what you saw beforehand affects the way your brain sees things now. In a similar way, when you look at impossible images all around you, it affects the way you see yourself.

Looking in the mirror you may not see yourself as you really are. But remind yourself that you and your body are amazing, whatever size or shape

WHAT CAN YOU DO?

So now you know that the images you see aren't real and that there's a risk they might affect you. And if they do, it can create a negative body image, and then that can make you feel bad and stop you doing things. So *what can you do about it?* GOOD QUESTION! Here's a three-part plan.

1. Train your brain

You've already learnt that many images we see aren't "real life", but your brain isn't really so easy to teach. You have a subconscious and a conscious brain. Over a long period of time, your subconscious brain has been trained into believing these fake images are real, so your conscious brain has to make a mindful effort to step in and say, "Whoa! Nobody looks like that!"

Only when you've practised a lot does something done by the conscious brain become subconscious. For example, when you learnt your times tables, it was HARD WORK. But the more you practised, the easier it became to answer 2 x 2 or 3 x 5 without thinking about it. You have to train your brain to use **media literacy**. This is a grand way of saying, "You can read images and understand their real meaning, not their fake meaning."

Of course there is nothing wrong with fun, cartoons, fantasy and dress up. The important thing is to train your eyes and mind like a superhero so that it doesn't affect the way you see yourself, and so that you keep up your positive body image.

Did you know that even you don't look like you in a photograph? So why think other people look like them? The lens of the camera distorts the picture. The processor of the camera highlights certain parts of your face and not others. If the colouring or light is bad, it makes the picture look bad, too. If you're moving, it might capture you in a strange moment. If you do a fun pose, people might think that's what you are like all the time, but of course you have lots of different sides to your personality. Most of all, a picture is not YOU. It's a two-dimensional image. And you are a three-dimensional human being with a personality.

QUESTIONS THAT **GOOD IMAGE DETECTIVES** ASK THEMSELVES

All the images in the media have one thing in common: someone created them. And they did it for a reason. Understanding these reasons helps us to understand the impact of the image on us. Every creator has their own ideas about the world, and that comes through in the pictures they create. Ask yourself:

- Who made the picture – a company? An individual? If so, who?
- Why did they make it? To sell something? To attract "likes"? To say this is the way to be beautiful?"
- Who is the picture for? Kids? Girls? Grown-ups?
- Does the image want you to do something differently? Do you want to do that?
- Does the image differ from what you might expect a normal person to look like? How? Why? Is it even realistic? And is anything left out?
- How does the image make you feel? Do you like the feeling or not? Why do you feel you need to pay attention to this image?
- Can you reject it if you want?

2. Eat good images

You've probably heard that what you eat affects your body, but what you LOOK AT also affects it. It's like your brain is eating all the images to develop its ideas about what people look like, and what it thinks about you. This is your VISUAL DIET. So a bad visual diet means back-to-front ideas about how you think you look. As though a rabbit did a wee in your soup and you drank it. (Please don't tell any grown-ups I talked aboutthis.) The point is, **make sure you're eating good images and having a healthy visual diet**.

3. Choose YOU, not blue

It's great to be happy and to spend time doing things you enjoy. To make sure this happens, you have to avoid getting into situations which make you feel blue about yourself. And YOU are the one that makes that choice. YOU decide if you are beautiful. YOU decide how to react to other people's opinions. YOU decide which images to look at. YOU decide whether they're real or not. YOU decide whether to stay home or go out and about.

It's quite normal to feel a bit blue once in a while. The best thing to do is to talk to a grown-up about it. And then do some of the things listed here:

- Think about all the amazing things your body can DO, from your skin, legs and tummy to your bottom (yes, bottoms are important!), eyes and cheeks.
- Don't let others hold you back – don't hide away at home but be out and about and be proud of your body and what you are doing with it!
- Make a note of how good you feel when you've actually done something and how your body played a part in that.
- Say something nice to someone else. Let someone else say nice things to you and BELIEVE THEM. Write down the compliments you are given. Go back and look at them. Remember to give yourself compliments, too!

- Your body is happier and healthier when YOU are happy and healthy. So love it, be kind to it, put good food in it and put happy thoughts about yourself into it.
- Spend more time looking at images that have not been manipulated so you can train your brain. More and more shops, websites and social media sites are using these. Try to read magazines, books and websites which focus on achievements rather than judging looks.
- If you do see some impossible images, it's perfectly okay as long as you remember it's just fantasy and your Very Impressive Brain (VIB) is on alert!
- Finally, make sure you're only serving up good images to your friends and family.

Feeling happy about the way you look is important, but it's just one part of your life. So why should it fill up everything you think about and do? There is so much to do – play an instrument, spend time with friends, learn to draw, go for a bike ride, read books, dance, spend time with your mum, tickle your tortoise... [insert all the activities here that you would like to do].

Your body shouldn't be the barrier to an exciting life, it should be the bridge! Your body is your machine and your weapon! And the best thing to do instead of feeling blue – go out there and make life happen! Don't let people's wrong ideas hold you back. Decide for yourself what to look like and do what you need to do!

"The most courageous act is still to think for yourself. Aloud."

COCO CHANEL

WHOSE OPINION IS IT ANYWAY?

Here are some big secrets no one ever tells you: nobody has the right to give you their opinion (even if they think they do). No one's opinion is any more right than anyone else's (even if they think it is). Other people's opinions might actually be completely wrong (they often are) and... here's the biggest secret... you don't have to actually pay any attention to their opinions anyway. You can decide your opinion about yourself, for yourself!

Every opinion comes with a point of view... but you don't need to agree with it. It took me until I was a grown-up to realise that just because someone says something, it doesn't make it true. And just because someone says something, they didn't necessarily mean it nicely (even if they say they are trying to be helpful). And what they say can be more about them than you.

Imagine this is you: a lovely happy sunshine, getting up every morning, shining your shine and getting on with your own business. You notice, out of the corner of your eye, a vampire hiding in a dark cave. The vampire looks unhappy and decides to offer his opinion to you about how awful he thinks you are: "Hi Sun. You are SO ugly, SO disgusting. You spread death and destruction wherever you smile your ridiculous yellow smile. I don't want to be anywhere near you, and nor should anyone else. I don't even know how you can stand to be you."

Can you think why the vampire has this opinion? Is it really true, and do you have to agree? Let's think about why the vampire has this opinion. Vampires are miserable and grumpy, and hide from the sun because it kills them. Just because the vampire thinks his opinion is right, doesn't mean you have to agree. In fact, you can think his opinion is completely wrong because you've thought about why he might have said it.

In exactly the same way, whenever you are given an opinion, think about the point of view of the person giving it. It will help you understand their perspective and decide if it is a useful opinion, why that person gave it to you, whether the opinion makes sense or not and whether to take any notice of it. **So when opinions come flying at you, you can decide for yourself whether they are valuable or not.**

When people give an opinion it can come in all different formats which might include words, memes, pictures, cartoons and facial expressions. Isn't it silly to stop yourself going out because of someone's opinion? Or holding yourself back because of a picture that was edited in an impossible way? Or someone else's idea? Or something that isn't even real? There's no point trying to be someone else's idea of an impossible image. That would be art. And art hangs in museums. Just hanging about all day. With other people looking at it. Just hanging on a wall. Going nowhere. Gathering dust. But you're a real person with real things to do!

Stay strong

All of the advice above might seem easier said than done. If someone gives an opinion about your looks and they sound confident, or bossy, you think they must be right. But that isn't true. Just think about all the people whose opinions in history were just cray-cray-crazy and sometimes downright dangerous. Despite knowing this, negative opinions can leave you questioning whether you are a valuable person. But what I know, and what you know now, is that how you look has nothing to do with what an amazing person you are. It's hard work when you have to keep reminding yourself that what people are saying might not be right. It takes practice but you can do it. Like a superhero that keeps having to fight off missiles. BAM! BAM! BAM! It's tiring, but you can do it.

Contradictory opinions

People often give opinions that contradict each other and even contradict themselves! I've heard the same people tell me one day that I'm too pale, and the next day that I'm dark. You might hear other contradictions, too – your hair is too short and too long. You should smile more and you should smile less. They might say wear make-up! And then they'll say it's not good to hide your skin. And it makes you think, HONESTLY JUST MAKE UP YOUR MIND.

But if you stop and think about it, all it means is that when they give an opinion about your looks, you don't need to pay any attention because it doesn't mean anything at all.

A PERSONAL NOTE

One of the things that affected my ideas of beauty as a child was opinions from people who felt they could tell me that I wasn't beautiful. Aunties and grown-ups would comment on my skin colour and my size and even tell me to my face that I wasn't beautiful! (That really hurt.)

Even now I'm a grown-up, people still feel like they can tell me that they don't like bits of me or think there are bits of me that aren't beautiful. And I get really upset when I hear grown-ups telling children the same hurtful things that were said to me. Sometimes children say things like that to each other, too. But wouldn't the world be much nicer if we were all kinder to each other?

A lot of the opinions I was given were just downright wrong. Wrong. Wrong. Wrong. WRONG. (You have to say that last bit in an up-down singsong kind of voice.) My skin colour is perfect as it is. I'm plenty beautiful and happy as I am. PLUS I'm an interesting person that does lots of interesting things! Well, I like to think so. And since it's my opinion, I'm sticking with it!

Is it true?

When you are given an opinion, think about the point of view of the person giving it. This will help you understand their perspective and decide if it is a useful opinion. My younger daughter gets upset because her big sister says, "You've got a stinky head made of marshmallows." Her sister tells her this to wind her up. As you can see, it works.

This is how the conversation goes:
Daughter (bawling her eyes out and crying very loudly): She said my head is stinky and it's made of marshmallows!
Me: Is your head stinky?
Daughter: No.
Me: Is your head made of marshmallows?
Daughter: No.
Me: So is it true that you have a stinky head made of marshmallows?
Daughter: But she said it!
Me: Just because she said it doesn't make it true. Why believe something you know isn't true?
Daughter: Humph.

So, if someone says something to you, the first thing to do is the **Stinky Marshmallow Head Test** and ask yourself, is it actually true?

Bank it or bin it?

If someone throws an opinion at you, don't let it splat you and knock you over. Use your force field to hold it at a distance and work out whether you should bank it or bin it. Is it a cabbage, rotten tomato or maybe a banana skin? Bin it. If it's a heart or a rose, then bank it!

Sometimes, people just want to be mean. That's called bullying. These comments have a big fat sticky label on them saying BIN IMMEDIATELY. DO NOT RECYCLE. Someone being mean could well have their own insecurities or problems. Maybe they're being bullied themselves. Maybe they're just repeating comments because they think it's cool. If someone says something mean, bin it. And walk off whistling your favourite sunshine tune.

Once in a while, a bad opinion is actually wrapped up in a good intention. The person might think they are trying to be helpful. You can think kindly about this person. But the opinion? Bin it!

Of course, when someone says something lovely, take the compliment! Maybe they like your style! They love how you've experimented with that look! Of course that unicorn onesie with the wellington boots and the alien antennae headband look good together! Your cheeks are flushed a gorgeous pink from all that energetic running! It's okay to feel good! Bank it, bank it, bank it. Enjoy sharing your powerful positive energy with the world. The more good energy you bank, the more beautiful you feel and the more good energy you have to share.

Use your opinion as a force for good

Just like the opinions of other people affect you, your opinions affect others. So use them wisely! You can help someone feel over the moon or down in the dumps. Celebrate people with your opinions. Try to find something positive to say – and make sure you mean it. And, as the famous saying goes, if you can't say anything nice, don't say anything at all. If you see someone giving their opinion and it's mean, you can intervene and point out that the opinion isn't kind, or perhaps isn't even true.

By saying everyone is beautiful – which is true anyway – and simply by thinking you and all the girls around you are beautiful, you are making the world a better place for all girls and women. **Just looking in the mirror and being happy with what you see is a revolutionary act!**

Your opinion of yourself

Now you've got KNOWLEDGE about how ideas about beauty are formed and why, the next step is to feel CONFIDENT in your opinion. Sometimes it's hard to get your tongue around the words so let's practise saying it: "*My* opinion is the most important. *My* opinion is the most important. And I am beautiful. I am beautiful. I am beautiful..." (Keep going till you run out of breath... keep going... keep going... keep going... phew!)

Trust your own ideas and decisions. Everyone has their own unique DNA, body, face and personality. Or to put it another way, you are your own unique YOU. And the best thing to be is to be YOU. YOU are BRILLIANT. YOU decide for yourself that YOU are BEAUTIFUL. How to be-**YOU**-tiful? The answer is in the question. **Be YOU.**

FIND YOUR STYLE

Your style is an important part of you. Style is about confidence, creativity and strong ideas about yourself. Your style is about how you express yourself and show your individuality. As the famous fashion designer Coco Chanel said, "Fashion fades, only style remains the same." There is no right or wrong style. Your style is what YOU want it to be.

Sometimes you want to stand out, but sometimes you want to fit in. Sometimes it's about being at the cutting edge of fashion, but sometimes the latest look is not for you. For some, fashion isn't a big deal, for others it's everything. Or something in between. It can even vary in importance at different stages of your life. Sometimes you can love a look, but then you give it your own twist. That's what makes it **YOUR** style.

Create your own style

Trying out different looks is like being an artist. You can take your inspiration from anywhere and create any style you like. Experimenting is important. Sometimes you get it right and sometimes you look back and think, "Why on Earth did I wear that?" That's how you develop your own style.

Ask a grown-up to show you their old photos and all the styles they tried out. You'll probably have a giggle over some of them, but fall in love with others. Maybe try out the latest fashions, or instead go for a vintage look. Upcycling old clothes can be stylish as well as environmentally friendly.

Different kinds of make-up, hairstyles, jewellery, headcoverings and even your shoes are part of your style and can be fun to experiment with. More permanent ways to change your look and style like tattoos, botox and plastic surgery need careful consideration. Copying someone else's style doesn't work because what suits one person's body and personality, doesn't suit another. You can be inspired by others, **but make it your own**.

It's more than just fashion and make-up

Style includes your self-expression, your confidence, how you own the room and your body language. Try out different ways to be expressive with your face and body. Do you smile or do you pout? It's up to you! Being brainy, smart and having an opinion for yourself are also brilliant style qualities. Don't forget, your style includes how you make other people feel. Be kind to others. Appreciate their unique style. COMPLIMENT THEM. Make positivity part of your style!

Do it for you

You shouldn't ever feel you have to wear certain clothes or make-up or look a certain way to fit in, or because someone else said so. Style means feeling comfortable with your heritage and culture, embracing your body, skin, face and hair type. They are what make you and your story. If you're confident in them, you'll have a winning style.

Whatever your approach, style is just one element of who you are. All the stories of the women in this book are about more than looks. They are stories about the impact they made on the world, which is about their own unique style. By being brave, creative and experimental, *you* could be the next big thing in style! Or science, or politics, or computers, or art, or space, or [insert name of dream job here]. All of these are about the style you bring to the world. I'm excited to see what you create, aren't you?

START A GIRL-POWERED REVOLUTION

Do you remember the story of Snow White? There's a bit where the Wicked Stepmother asks the mirror, "Who's the fairest of them all?" At that moment, we're all rooting for Snow White to be announced as the most beautiful. But only recently did I stop to ask myself, why does the storyteller think being beautiful is the most important part of the story?

Maybe the Wicked Stepmother wasn't wicked after all, but instead people had made her feel bad all her life about her looks, as though that was the only important thing about her. If only she could have read this book! But then I thought an even bigger thought – **being beautiful is not a competition because we are all beautiful! The most important thing is to be yourself.** And instead of a competition, we can support each other just like Snow White and the Stepmother could have. Which would have made for a much happier ending!

You can stop listening to all those voices that tell you how to look and that make you feel bad. Instead, you can decide for yourself. As a girl deciding your own opinion about beauty, you are carrying out a revolutionary act, changing everyone's world for the better! On this exciting new journey, you can seek out new, beautiful images, experiment with styles, looks and ideas, even get inspiration from history, grown-ups, art and fashion. You can learn the real-life stories of amazing women beyond their looks. Maybe one day your story will be included as one of them.

Put on your heart glasses

It's **you** that decides what is beautiful and makes it so. And that's the whole point of this book – to recalibrate your eyes to see the beauty that is in yourself and is all around you. **You can choose to see beautifully.** Once you've put on your "heart glasses", it will change how you see the world and yourself. It will take time to get the toxic beauty ideals and negative voices out of your system. But by **making a promise to yourself** to keep going, you'll start to see how much beauty is around you, and in yourself.

Eating **a better visual diet** will help. So will **choosing to be you not blue**. But most of all, realising that you no longer need to accept other people's ideas of what it means to be beautiful will dramatically change how you feel about yourself.

Make yourself a promise

Here's mine: *I promise to wear my heart glasses whenever I look at myself and the people around me and to see the beauty in who we are. Not what others tell me. I'll work hard to make sure all of us believe we are beautiful.*

Write your own promise to yourself here, where you can look back at it often:

How to beYOUtiful

The most important part of believing **"I am beautiful"** is feeling it's true in the bottom of your heart. Many people (including grown-ups) find it difficult to say it and **really believe it**.

Let's practise. Say: "I am beautiful" now. (I'm doing it, too!) You can whisper it or even shout it out loud at the top of your lungs! You can also try: "We are all beautiful." (I love this sentence!) And the best part about it is that it is true.

You are beautiful, I am beautiful, and so is the person next to you. (You can nudge them and tell them that. I hope they've been saying it, too!) **Remember, believing you are beautiful is the most beautiful thing of all.**

GLOSSARY

ADOPTION – When a child is brought up by parent(s) who are not their birth parents

BEAUTY IDEAL – Someone's idea of the correct way to be beautiful

BODY IMAGE – Your feelings about the way your body looks

BODY LANGUAGE – How you communicate through your body and its movements

BODY SHAPE – A way to describe the form or outline of your body. Often words like "hourglass" or "pear" are used

CHEMOTHERAPY – The use of special chemicals to treat illnesses like cancer

CLEFT LIP – A gap or split in the upper lip that people are born with

COLOURISM – Prejudice against people with darker skin tones of the same skin colour. Sometimes it is called shadeism

CORSET – A stiff, tight undergarment worn to shape the middle part of the body, usually to make it look smaller

CULTURE – The characteristics and social behaviours of a group of people including things like their ideas, traditions, customs, language, food and art

DISCRIMINATION – Treating someone unfairly, especially because of their race, age or sex

DIVERSITY – Many different types of things or people being included in something

DNA – The material in cells that carries all the information about how a living thing will look and function

DWARFISM – A medical condition that restricts body growth

(THE) ESTABLISHMENT – The people in control of society or government

FEMININITY – Characteristics traditionally associated with being female

GENETIC VARIATION – The difference in DNA among individuals that creates different physical characteristics

HERITAGE – Something that comes from your family, culture or society's background, often to do with your ethnic origin

124

INDIVIDUALITY – The qualities of a person that make them different from others

INFLUENCER – A person who is perceived to have the power to affect the opinions and behaviours of many people. Usually refers to people with a big social media following

MELANIN – A natural pigment that gives colour to hair, skin and eyes in humans and animals

MENINGOCOCCAL SEPTICAEMIA – An infection of the bloodstream that causes blood poisoning

PERSONALITY – The combination of qualities that make up a person's unique character

PIGMENT – Something that gives colour to another material or object

PREHISTORIC – From the time before written history

PROPORTIONS – The relationship between the size of different things

PROSTHETIC – Artificial body part

PUBERTY – When a child's body starts to change as they become an adult

RACISM – When someone is treated differently because of their race, ethnicity, nationality or colour. Usually this refers to prejudice, discrimination or hatred

RADICAL – Really huge or extreme

REPRESENTATION – The act of ensuring all different kinds of people are presented to audiences

REVOLUTION – A very great change or overthrow of the way things have previously been done

SELF-CONSCIOUS – Overly sensitive of yourself and your image

SOCIAL STATUS – The rank someone holds in society, based on factors like wealth, power and influence

TUXEDO – A black jacket, trousers, special white shirt and bow tie, worn for formal occasions, usually by men

VISUAL DIET – The collection of images that are viewed and enter the brain

VOLUPTUOUS – A body shape with curves

INDEX

FURTHER INFORMATION

Be Real: Body Confidence for Everyone
A campaign and resources to help people be body confident and change attitudes to body image, putting health above appearance.
www.berealcampaign.co.uk

Girlguiding: Free Being Me
A body confidence programme to help girls recognise myths about how they "should" look and how to be happy in their own skin.
www.girlguiding.org.uk/making-guiding-happen/programme-and-activities/peer-education/what-is-peer-education/free-being-me

Mediasmart
Supporting media literacy in children with resources and parent guides on subjects like social media and body image, with a focus on the advertising industry.
www.mediasmart.uk.com

This Girl Can
A campaign to get more women and girls active without worrying about what others think.
www.thisgirlcan.co.uk

Young Minds: Body Image
The UK's leading charity championing well-being and mental health of young people, including body image in children.
www.youngminds.org.uk/young-person/coping-with-life/BODY-IMAGE

Common Sense Media
An organisation that focuses on digital well-being for kids, with resources for parents and children to make healthy choices about entertainment and technology based on reviews and guidance.
www.commonsensemedia.org

Dove Evolution video
Watch a video showing how a model is made over, and the picture is adjusted to create a new image.
www.youtube.com/watch?v=iYhCn0jf46U

Childline
A free, private and confidential online or telephone service for under 19s to talk about any issue they're going through.
Call 0800 1111 or go to *www.childline.org.uk*